Elisabeth Donati

MONEY...

THE INSTRUCTION MANUAL

The easiest way to prepare

KIDS & TEENS

to handle money like a pro when they get older!

FOR AGES 10 & UP!

For more information about our unique approach to teaching financial education, and life, to kids, teens and the adults who love them, please visit www.CreativeWealthIntl.org. Thank you for your support.

Elisabeth Donati

"The Financial Literacy Lady"

Additional financial education resources for kids and teens:

- The Ultimate Allowance (for parents)

- Rock to Riches (for kids)

- The Money Jars: Your Magical Money Management System

- Financial Wisdom Coloring Book for Kids & Parents

- Camp Millionaire Camp and School Curriculum

- Moving Out for Teens Camp and School Curriculum

- The Money Game (home and school use)

InnerWealth Publishing

Whitefish, MT 59937

805-957-1024 • Fax: 888-408-1579

www.CreativeWealthIntl.org • info@CreativeWealthIntl.org

TABLE OF CONTENTS

© 2021 InnerWealth Publishing

BONUS FOR YOU!

Our biggest goal is for you to be wildly successful at creating financially responsible adult humans who can think for, and make empowering decisions for, him or herself.

The following additional resources are available for you to use with your family. We want to do everything in our power to help you create financially savvy adults who contribute to the world they live in.

Here's what you get...

- **Electronic Version of the book** so you can print out additional workbook pages for additional children if you purchased the print version.

- **Money Jars: Your Magical Money Management System** e-book to learn more about The Money Jar, how to set them up, answers to common questions, etc.

- **Creative Wealth Money Principle Cards for Kids** - Our 30 financial principles to print on card stock, cut and review.

- **Being Older Visualization** to use with your kids and teens.

- **Money Habits Worksheet** to print and use as you and your children learn.

- **Golden Goose Story** to read to your children.

- A list of what else you can do!

Whether you purchased this book on Amazon or as a PDF/downloadable e-book from our website, simply go here to get access your bonuses:

http://moneybookforkids.com/bonus-page

Note: if you purchased the book on Amazon, please have your order number available when you sign up to access the bonuses.

See you inside the portal!

A NOTE TO PARENTS / GUARDIANS / TEACHERS

If you're like most parents, making sure your kids grow into adults who can take care of themselves financially is a priority. That's why you're investing your valuable time and energy into their financial education.

The world is an interesting place now, with the move toward more and more technology, more automation, more people working from home, more disparity between low level/low paying jobs and high level/high paying positions.

There are many reasons to prepare our children to be financially successful...

- We want them to be able to create and enjoy the greatest life possible.
- We want them to be resourceful, not hopeless or helpless.
- We need them to not want or need to count on us to take care of them later.
- We want to save them from having to learn financial lessons the hard way, like so many of us have had to do.
- We want them not to have to move back in with us later, unless WE want them to!

Did any of those reasons strike a cord with you? Regardless of the motivation behind training your kids to be financially savvy adults, you get points! The more financially independent adults we create in the world, the fewer people we have dependent on 'the system'...and as we all know, that system is struggling in innumerable ways.

A little bit about "*Money...The Instruction Manual*"

We created this financial education workbook for parents and kids to enjoy together. Our goal is to provide an environment that encourages conversation between every member of your household. It's only through open communication that kids and adults can share how they feel about money, how to use money, teach each other what they've learned through personal experience and begin to learn that talking about money is not a taboo but essential for a healthy financial adulthood.

Bottom line...it's simply time to start talking about money!

Another objective is to help you create a financial education foundation for your children to build upon as they get older. The financial topics are endless, but without a basic understanding of money and wealth creation, it's virtually impossible to learn, let alone apply, more challenging financial strategies.

This book is an powerful financial education tool to use and enjoy with your whole family. We've made it user-friendly and haven't assumed that you are familiar with the financial terminology and principles in the book. After all, chances are YOU never learned about money as a child, either. If you need to look up a term, simply refer to the comprehensive glossary in the back of the book to learn more or do additional research on the web, and don't forget YouTube. It is an endless source of great financial education material. One of my favorite's on YouTube is called *Money As Debt*. Please watch it with your child(ren).

Please know that raising money savvy adults takes more than simply going through this cool financial education book (though it's a GREAT start). To make sure your kids can handle money responsibly when they move out AND thrive on their own financially, we recommend the following three important steps.

FIRST, remember that your children are learning about money by watching, listening and experiencing (physically and emotionally) everything YOU and other adults in their lives are doing with money (this applies equally to other aspects of life, as well).

> *"Children have never been very good at listening to their elders, but they have never failed to imitate them."* — James Baldwin

This means that you must be willing to set the very best example you can, in all areas of life, not just financially. If you haven't learned about money yet or are just getting started, in our experience, kids appreciate knowing their parents aren't perfect and don't know everything. Just tell them you're going to learn about money as a family!

> *"Setting an example is not the main means of influencing others, it is the only means."* — Albert Einstein

SECOND, expose your child to every aspect of your family's financial life. Talk to them about the family budget, income, expenses, savings, investments, credit cards, bank account, insurance, donations...if it has to do with money, involve them.

Contrary to popular belief, you are NOT burdening your children. They are curious about life and adulthood as they older and WANT to know. Not only that but they NEED to know. They MUST understand the financial aspect of being an adult if you want them to be responsible adults. Remember that it's your job to teach them how to be adults and there's no better way than to make sure they understand money than to expose them to every aspect of it as a child and teen.

We also suggest you talk to them about your financial challenges. This tells them it's OK to have challenges with money as an adult...because they will...we all do.

Have your kids help you review and pay bills and credit cards online, write checks, look over utility bills, insurance policies, bank statements, investment portfolios if you have them. If you buy a house or a car, take your children with you, let them see the paperwork, let them ask the salesperson questions. It's all great experience for later.

And by all means, invite them to be an integral part of the family's planning and budgeting, especially for vacations, college expenses, purchases the whole family will benefit from, investments for retirement, etc. They have to see what it takes to run a family, and I repeat, it's OK that you don't have it all together. It's more important that you tell the truth so they see money honestly through your eyes than make something up that confuses them. Children always know when we're not telling them the truth!

In order to change the cultural taboo around talking about money, we must retrain ourselves and train our kids to view money as a tool to reach their dreams, a tool to create the life they want, a tool for becoming financially free, a tool for accomplishing great things, a tool for helping other people reach their dreams, and of course, a tool to do a lot of good in the world.

By talking openly with your kids (and your kids' friends) about money, you begin to dispel this taboo and show kids that it's OK to talk about money...even more so, it's critical that they do so.

THIRD, remember that we don't get good at anything without a lot of practice! I strongly encourage you to provide your child with an allowance...but not just any type of allowance...give them *The ULTIMATE Allowance*. I wrote this book years ago to help parents prepare their kids to handle money wisely.

The Ultimate Allowance shows you how to take the money you're already spending ON your children and run it THROUGH them instead. The older they get, the more areas of spending they become responsible for so that by the time they are ready to leave home, they understand how to manage, save and spend money responsibly.

The Ultimate Allowance is a great addition to this program. You can purchase the printed or Kindle version on Amazon and the PDF version at www.FinancialEducationStore.com.

OK, let's get your children prepared to handle money wisely!

HOW TO USE THIS BOOK

This book has been designed to:

1) Help you and your children learn, understand and feel comfortable with the language of money, financial principles, investing concepts and money habits, along with the mental and emotional aspects of money, and more.

2) Guide you through teaching the material to your children in a way that we hope will stimulate thoughtful conversation, and action plans with regard to their futures and the many roles money plays in their lives.

If there's one thing I've discovered about teaching kids and teens, it's that they often take what I tell them verbatim and literally. They have no reason to doubt me. If I hand a child a glass half filled with water and tell him it's a glass half filled with water, he will simply say, "OK."

On the other hand, if I hand that same glass to an adult, he will question me and give me reasons why he doesn't necessarily believe it's really a glass half filled with water.

This is partly because children tend to trust us (unless they have been lied to or abused in some way) and partly because they haven't developed a whole host of stories, beliefs, and perceptions about why things are or aren't how and what they seem (I know you understand what I mean).

We approach the subject of money as a game that *anyone* can win, as long as you learn, understand and use the rules correctly and regularly. We also know that the rules of money change over time. This is where life-long learning comes into play. You can't just learn once and stop learning. You must constantly educate yourself financially.

There's nothing new or mysterious about the money principles in this workbook... they have been used since the beginning of time by financial savvy adults. They are incorporated in all of the financial camps and games I developed, including Camp Millionaire, The Money Camp and The Money Game.

The main, and most important, principle is simply save a portion of every dollar you make and invest it wisely in assets, generally for a long period of time and voila...you usually create financial freedom! It takes a lot of trial and error and a lot of learning and making mistakes. In the end though, the goal of becoming financially free and secure is reachable for virtually everyone. (And yes, there are many human beings who aren't capable of doing this for themselves. This is why the program stresses donation and helping others as part of all important financial plans.)

In addition to investing for the long run, another important financial principle involves teaching kids to invest in different types of assets that produce ongoing cash flow. Because the appreciation of different types of assets go up and down over time, it's important to have investment money in several types of assets. This is where the principle, "Don't put all of your money into one basket," comes from! More on this later!

There are so many ways to invest your financial freedom (retirement/investment) money, but we'll leave that for another day. Suffice it to say, the entrepreneurial approach of generating ongoing cash flow is a far more empowering approach when it comes to helping kids turn into adults who can really take creating financial freedom for themselves seriously.

After going through *Money...The Instruction Manual* with your kids and teens, encourage them to read and learn more in areas where they showed the greatest interest.

TIP: I highly suggest that you PAY your children (yes, you read that correctly) to read financial and entrepreneurship books. Require a short written report on each chapter and have a conversation with them about what they learned from the book and how they can use it now, and in the future, before they get paid for reading the book. Extra credit points if you make them write the report by hand so they can practice their handwriting because YES, it's getting harder and harder to read people's writing.

And lastly, remember to use situations that occur in everyday life as opportunities to more deeply explore how money works. The time you take to do this with your children will pay huge rewards in their futures.

How the book is formatted:

The book has been divided into the following areas:

1) Thinking about money

2) Earning vs. Making money

3) Managing money

4) Spending money

5) Saving money

6) Investing money

7) Donating money

The parent or teacher portion on the left side of the book is broken down into five areas. You'll get the hang of it after a couple of pages.

1) The PRINCIPLES

2) The WHAT

3) The WHY

4) The HOW

5) Additional comments

6) Vocabulary words

Feel free to teach additional information that you know well, add personal and other related stories and let your child lead you in exploring other areas that they may have questions about. Our goal is to keep the information simple...but relevant and again, to get your whole family talking about money!

If there is anything you don't understand, or simply want further clarification on, please feel free to give me a call at 805-637-7888 or send me an email at elisabethdonati@gmail.com. YES, those are my real numbers. I want to be able to help you!

I am here to support you in the important process of preparing your children for adulthood. I wish you fabulous success in this beautiful process! And as always, remember to *Pay Yourself First!*

Elisabeth Donati

Elisabeth Donati
Your Financial Literacy Lady

WHY LEARN ABOUT MONEY	
Principle/ Lesson:	People only learn and remember what's relevant, otherwise it's irrelevant. To be financially successful, learn the language of money.
What:	Get your child to understand why it's important to learn about money when they are younger, rather than waiting until they are older.
Why:	In order for anyone to want to learn, they have to see it as relevant to their lives at the time or in the future. Children are no different. We've also learned, and we're sure you already know, that it's challenging to get kids to think past what's for dessert tonight at dinner. Getting them to contemplate their future, whether it's one year, five years or 40 years away, can bewilder even the most creative child. They just aren't ready to go there yet (and we can hardly blame them!). If we want them to learn the value of money, how to use it wisely and how to make it grow to help them be financially free, we must help them find a way to relate it to their current lives as well as get them to begin thinking about it in terms of their future happiness and success as a human being. As parents, you understand the developing passions and talents of your children better than anyone. Find ways to relate the Creative Wealth Principles and concepts to these passions and talents in a way that helps them understand the material and you will help prepare them for a future of freedom and security that is available to everyone.
How:	Simply ask your child the questions on the following page. Most kids by the age of 6 or 7 are very aware of money, what it buys, how to get it out of the bank, etc. We want them to think about money in terms of a resource that will help them reach their dreams as adults. It's important that they begin to establish positive money habits that will follow them into adulthood. The sooner they begin these habits, the more likely they are to succeed.
Comments/ Extra activities:	Walk your child through a simple visualization of being an older person. Ask him to close his eyes, see himself very old. Ask him what he is wearing, what he is doing, how healthy he is, things like that. Then, ask him to think about all of the choices and decisions he made with money in order to be able to live comfortably as his older self. Remind him that an older version of himself is always depending on him to make wise choices now and in the future.
Vocabulary:	Money, financial freedom.

WHY LEARN ABOUT MONEY?

List all the reasons why you should learn **how money works**?

_____

_____

_____

_____

_____

List some things **you** want to learn about money?

_____

_____

_____

_____

_____

When is the best time to learn about money?

_____

_____

(Answer: As soon as possible!!!)

ASK YOUR PARENTS	
Principle/ Lesson:	Talking about money is easy and perfectly OK. Money is energy to be used as a tool to create financial freedom.
What:	Open, honest communication, as well as watching the examples you set for your children, are some of the most important ways they learn from you. This exercise gives you some talking points to start having great conversations about money and wealth with your children. These questions will help your entire family begin to feel comfortable talking about money and creating wealth for the family.
Why:	The most common reason for divorce in the US is disagreement over money because spouses usually have different money personalities or blueprints (read *Secrets of the Millionaire Mind* by T. Harv Eker). In addition, there is a huge cultural taboo when it comes to families talking about money and money issues. It's critically important that we have conversations about money in a non judgmental fashion. Let your child see what's going on, hear you talk about money, be part of the decision-making process in terms of budgeting, planning for vacations, researching investment opportunities, etc.
How:	Simply allow your child(ren) to ask you the questions on the following page. Answer them honestly and without emotion. As soon as you and your child begin to see money simply as energy (i.e., a resource or tool) that can be used for all sorts of great things, the sooner he will begin to find ways to accumulate this energy for himself.
Comments/ Extra activities:	While we encourage you to share all the family's financial information with your child, you can also request that your child not share this information with friends and neighbors, or use it as a way to feel 'better than' others who may not have as much money, or conversely, to feel embarrassment or shame if you have less than others. This is where the concept of money as energy becomes so valuable. You will have many opportunities to talk about money simply being a resource or tool; money isn't good or bad or right or wrong. Just like electricity, it all depends on how you use it. Remember, many of these conversations will bring up your own personal issues as a adult and parent so be prepared to explore what money means for you as well. The book mentioned above is a great resource for your own personal growth in relationship to money.
Vocabulary:	Managing money, financial freedom, retirement, investment.

ASK YOUR PARENTS

Why do your parents want you to learn about money?

_____

_____

How did your parents learn how money worked?

_____

_____

How did your parents learn about managing their money?

_____

_____

How do your parents keep track of their money?

_____

_____

What does 'financial freedom' mean to your parents?

_____

_____

What does 'retirement' mean to your parents?

_____

_____

What was your parents worst investment?_____

What was your parents best investment? _____

What would your parents change if they could start over financially?

_____

_____

What else would you like to know about your family's financial situation and money?

_____

_____

FINANCIAL FREEDOM ROAD MAP	
Principle/ Lesson:	If you don't know where you're going, any road will take you there.
What:	The Financial Freedom Road Map is a visual representation of the tools we can use to reach financial freedom.
Why:	As the saying on the bottom of the page indicates, it's impossible to know how to get where you're going unless you KNOW where you're going. Most people don't get what they want because they don't know what they want. The word "freedom" is powerful for both kids and adults so we want them to begin to associate "money" with "freedom" in terms of making choices that involve money which lead to freedom not dependency.
How:	Starting at "Start Here", go over the steps along the way to Financial Freedom, explaining that these are some of the areas and concepts they will be learning. Explain to them that there are as many ways to become financially free as there are people. Each person has to find the way that works for them.
Comments/ Extra activities:	Share with your kids the areas you are comfortable with and the areas you need/want to learn more about. If you're like most adults, life's 'To Do' lists often get in the way of learning more in the area of investing and wealth creation. Let your kids help motivate you toward learning more about investing for yourself and as a family.
Vocabulary:	Road map, money game, money jars, spending, stock market, business, real estate, invest.

Start Here

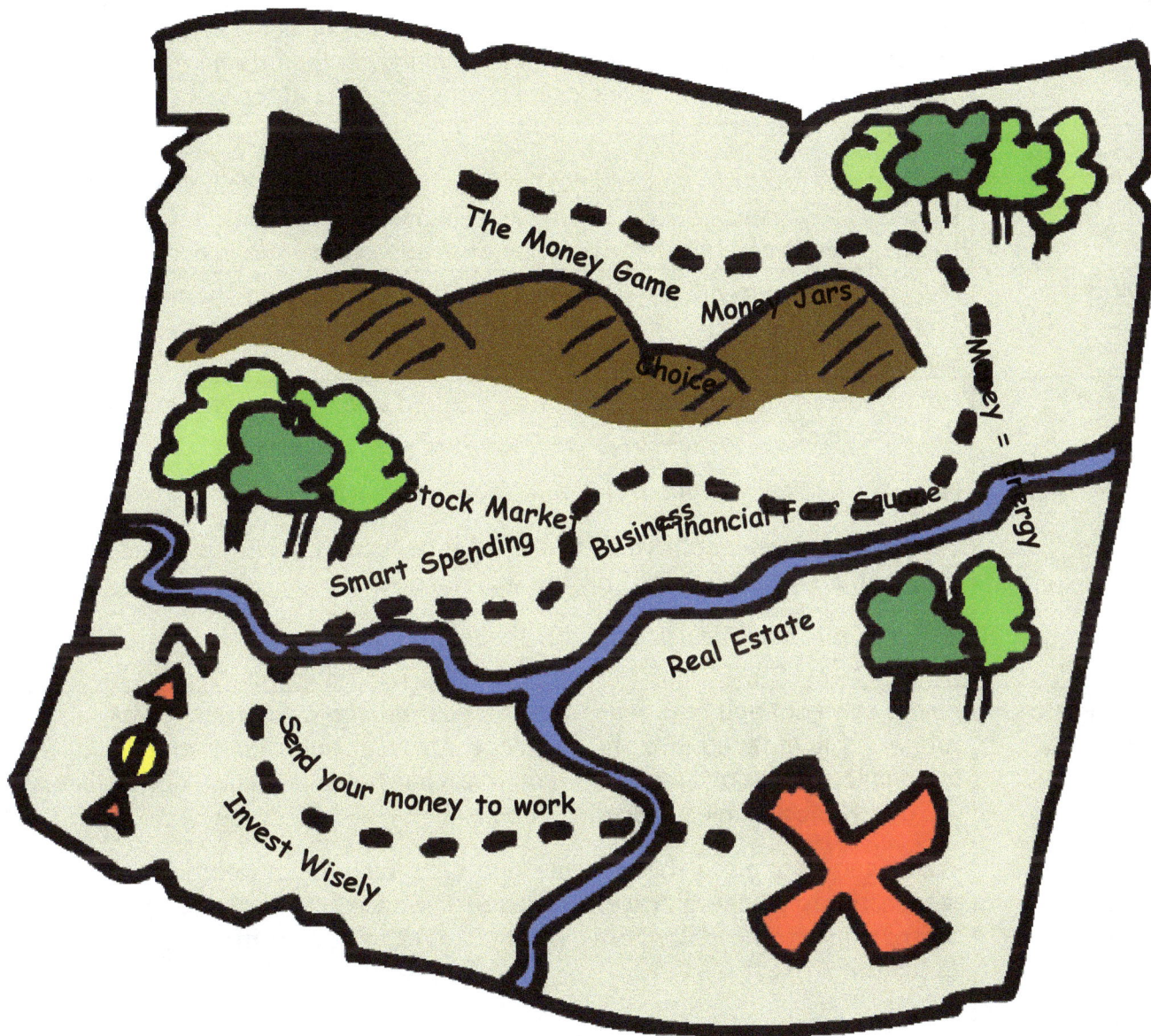

The Money Game
Money Jars
Choices
Money = Energy
Stock Market
Smart Spending
Business
Financial Fear Square
Real Estate
Send your money to work
Invest Wisely

Your Goal...Financial Freedom

*"If you don't know where you're going,
any road will take you there!"*

THE CONTRACT	
Principle/ Lesson:	If it sounds too good to be true, it often is. Read the fine print before you sign on the dotted line.
What:	A contract is an agreement between you and either another person, group of people or business entity. You are agreeing to the information written in the contract and there are usually consequences attached to NOT abiding by the contract. Also, if you find that you can not fulfill a contract or accomplish or stick to what you agreed to, you can often renegotiate the contract. The key is to be up front and honest with whomever you signed the contract.
Why:	Many, if not most, adults sign contracts without reading them thoroughly. It's important to take the time needed to know exactly what you're agreeing to and putting your signature on.
How:	Have your child read through the agreements and have him sign and date the agreement if he finds 1, 2, & 3 acceptable. Note: If he really reads it, he will object to number 2! Have a discussion about what might have happened if he had signed this contract without reading it all the way through. Ask him, or have him ask you, the three questions under the definition of CONTRACT.
Comments/ Extra activities:	Find a contract you have signed in the past and go over what it was for, why you entered into the contract, etc. Mention that even having telephone service or electricity run into your home is a contract between you and the companies providing the service. Have your child go to the internet and type in contract and do some research into all the different types of contracts, who writes up contracts (attorneys/lawyers), what it costs to have contracts written up (drawn up), etc.
Vocabulary:	Contract, agreement, attorney, lawyer.

THE CONTRACT

"In order to succeed, we must first believe we can!"
...author unknown

I, _____ (print name here), agree to the following:

1. I agree to share the financial information, principles and habits I learn in Money... The Instruction Manual with my family and friends who are interested in financial independence.

2. I agree to lick the bottom of my dinner plate every night for a month.

3. Learning and using the information in Money...The Instructional Manual is up to me and I take 100% responsibility for creating financial freedom in my life.

In exchange for the agreements above, the Creative Wealth Team promises to teach you the information you need to know to grow up and become financially free.

Camper Signature:_____ Date: _____

CONTRACT — A formal agreement (usually written) between two or more people or companies. Your signature on a contract **USUALLY** makes it legal so read what you sign **BEFORE** you sign it!

Question 1: If a contract isn't signed, does that mean it isn't legal?

Question 2: If a contract is signed, does that mean it's always legal?

Question 3: If two people agree to something verbally, is it legal if there's no signed agreement?

Answers: 1) Not necessarily   2) No   3) It may be, it may not be

All three of these questions depend on the situation and are often decided in a court of law.

Moral...do your best to know exactly what you're agreeing to and always seek legal advice from a qualified attorney!

YOUR MONEY DECLARATIONS	
Principle/ Lesson:	Your life is a result of your thoughts, beliefs, attitudes and habits. What you focus on expands. Thoughts are things. What we think about we bring about.
What:	Declarations are a way of energetically programming certain beliefs and ideas into our minds. Declarations help reinforce new ideas and concepts and increase the chances that you and your child will learn and incorporate these new ideas and concepts into your daily lives.
Why:	As adults, most of us have had the experience of attending a seminar or class and getting all excited about the new information, concepts, ideas, processes, etc., that we've learned. However, all too often, this positive experience is followed by brief application and is then relegated to that 'seminar shelf' in your bookcase, never to be looked at or used again. Declarations are a way to reinforce learning and instill new behaviors because saying these declarations out loud produces a vibratory response in the body that helps lock in the learning.
How:	Both you and your child, and whole family if available, stand up, place your hand over your heart (remind you of the Pledge of Allegiance?) and say the declarations on the opposite page out loud, feeling the vibrations of your voice in your hand. Say these declarations before and after each daily lesson, regardless of how many pages you worked through. Power tip: You can say the declarations with emphasis on different parts of the declaration. Example: "I" always pay myself first vs. I ALWAYS pay myself first vs. I always PAY myself first. You get the idea. Have fun with them!
Comments/ Extra activities:	Make up additional declarations for other areas of life: health, sports, school, music, etc.
Vocabulary:	Declaration, beliefs, attitudes.

YOUR MONEY DECLARATIONS

I play the money game to win.

I am the CEO of my own life.

My thoughts, beliefs and attitudes determine my financial future.

I work because I want to, not because I have to.

I get what I want because I know what I want.

I choose how to earn or make my money.

I am an excellent money manager.

I only borrow money when it's going to make me money.

I save up my money to buy the things I want.

I spend my money wisely.

I always pay myself first.

I spend less money than I make.

Interest is only interesting when I'm receiving it.

I put my money to work for me.

I save early and I save often!

I invest my money wisely.

I choose to be financially free!

THE MONEY QUIZ

| Principle/ Lesson: | Financial freedom is your choice.

I choose to be financially free. |
|---|---|
| What: | The life you create for yourself is essentially the sum of all of the choices you make over the course of your lifetime. |
| Why: | Most people, when asked, never remember having made a conscious choice to grow up and be financially free. Most people function as 'firefighters' instead of 'architects', spending their days reacting to situations that happen 'to' them instead of 'creating' the lives they want by attracting situations into their lives that lead to their goals.

In order to create a life of freedom, (or creativity or service or love, for example) you first have to know you can and must choose it for yourself, go through the conscious act of making the choice and then follow up with the steps needed to make it happen.

It's also important to understand that when you say Yes to one choice you are always saying No to other choices and on an even deeper level, it's important to teach this next generation to think past how their desired choice affects them to how it affects their community, their state, and even the world. There are no isolated choices. |
| How: | Read the first sentence and then have your child choose one of the three options. Explain that most people aren't taught to make conscious choices and that even when they don't think they've made a choice, they have actually made the choice to stay exactly where they are.

There is a saying...If you always do what you've always done, you always get what you've always gotten. In order to GET something different than what you've already gotten, you have to CHOOSE something different and then take the steps necessary to make it happen. All this means is that you must choose to grow up and have plenty of money if that's what you want. |
| Comments/ Extra activities: | Discuss whether or not you ever made the choice to be financially free and if so, how did that choice affect your decisions, behaviors, and finally what resulted from the decision?

If you didn't make that choice, how did NOT making the choice affect your decisions? |
| Vocabulary: | Choices. |

Answer the following question (check the right box):

I'd like to grow up and ...

❏ Not have enough money to live comfortably.

❏ Have just enough money to pay for the things I need.

❏ Have plenty of money to live the lifestyle I choose.

Financial Freedom happens because...

YOU Choose It!
YOU Make It Happen!

"When you never choose, you lose!"

In other words, by NOT making a choice, you make a choice to stay where you are, doing what you're doing, getting the results you're getting.

If it's to be, it's up to ME!

I CAN'T WAIT TO GROW UP	
Principle/ Lesson:	Growing up happens quicker than you think. "Tell me, what is it you plan to do with your wild and precious life?" – Mary Oliver
What:	There's lots of firsts in life and many of those firsts are age-related. This chart gives kids the opportunity to see what kinds of things happen at what ages and also that many events can happen at many different ages. While it's important to learn to be present in life, it's also good to know what may be coming up and do a little planning for it.
Why:	This chart is designed to get the kids to role play being different ages so they can begin to get an idea of what life events to expect at what ages. Most of the time, kids really don't know what's coming as they get older and hopefully, wiser. This activity let's them explore the future for a bit, ask questions and imagine where they might be at certain ages.
How:	Go through the list on the bottom of the chart and put every event in every square where it might fit. It's fine to put more than one event in each square. Ask your child who they know who has experienced each event and have them explore what it might have been like to have experienced it. Have them think about all of the things that you might have to do to prepare for a few of the events, for example, what might lead up to getting your first car or having your first home.
Comments/ Extra activities:	Ask your child to come up with additional life events they can place in the squares.
Vocabulary:	License, diploma, retirement, investment, passport.

I CAN'T WAIT TO GROW UP

Ages 10-22	Ages 23-30	Ages 31-50	Ages 51 up

POSSIBLE LIFE EVENTS

Driver's License

First Savings Account

First Car

High School Diploma

First Checking Account

First Apartment

Register to Vote

College Graduation

First Job

First Marriage

First Credit Card

Having Children

Saving for Kid's College

First Home

Make first million dollars

Real Estate

Career Change

First Investments

Health Issues

Parent's Health Issues

Parent's Retirement

Your Retirement

First Solo Vacation

Start First Business

Get Passport

THE MONEY GAME	
Principle/ Lesson:	I play the money game to win. Using money is like a game. It has a ball, rules, coaches, fans, team players, a field and a snack bar. Anyone can learn to win the money game.
What:	Earning, making, spending, saving, investing and donating are all parts to the great game we call The Money Game, but you have to know and use the rules (on a regular basis) to win.
Why:	Many people are uncomfortable talking about their own personal financial situations because they've grown up thinking the amount of money they have or the kind of fancy 'stuff' they have makes a difference in who they are and who others think they are. It's critical that kids learn that money doesn't 'mean' anything about who they are as people. Learning to think of money as a game can set a comfortable tone for kids to begin talking with you or their peers about money. Most people play the money game <u>not to lose</u>; they play defensively instead of offensively. We want kids to play the money game offensively, consciously making decisions that lead to financial freedom instead of stress and struggle.
How:	Have your child read each sentence, then ask questions relative to something he is interested in, e.g., relate to baseball if he is into baseball, relate to a band if she plays the flute, etc. Make it relevant to their lives When he get to the bottom of the page, see if he can figure out what's missing (the rules) and let him fill in the sentence, "I play the money game to win.".
Comments/ Extra activities:	Have your child choose a Coach, Team Players, Fans, Stadium and finally ask them what would be in their Snack Bar. Talk about why these things are important and why he would choose these people.
Vocabulary:	Money game, principles, financial coach/mentor.

What you need to Win the Money Game...

You have a Financial Coach/Mentor (financial advisor or planner) but you can also learn how to be your own Coach!

You have a Ball (the energy of money)

You have Team Players
(bosses, co-workers, employees)

You have Fans (family, friends, supporters)

You have a Stadium
(where you play the game)

You have a Snack Bar
(enjoying and sharing the great things in life)

What's Missing Here? _ _ _ _ _ _ _ _!
(a.k.a. The Creative Wealth Principles)

"I play THE MONEY GAME to _ _ _!"

HOW MONEY WORKS

Principle/ Lesson:	You have to know the rules of the money game to win the money game. All wealth is learned.
What:	Creative Wealth Principles are simply the rules to The Money Game. It's important to know the rules if you want to win the game. Unlike a baseball game, everyone CAN win The Money Game and it's important for your child to understand this, even if you don't believe it yet. NOTE: Many people are under the assumption and false belief that there is a limited amount of money in the world. While it is true that there are a limited number of dollar bills in the world at any given time, the amount of 'value' that can be created by human beings is unlimited. There IS enough to go around and the fact that one person has a lot money has nothing to do with whether or not another person can also have a lot of money. Also, please keep in mind that one of our goals for this manual is to expose kids and teens to the philosophies that making money while doing good and making lots of money in order to donate and do good in the world are what tend to provide life satisfaction for most people.
Why:	Kids rarely learn about money and wealth creation in school or at home. YOU are breaking this cycle by making sure your kids have a clue! Thank you for that. Kids must learn how to play the money game because unless they are willing to participate fully, it can be quite challenging to be financially secure as an adult.
How:	Have them attempt to fill in the blanks. Then, go over each one and help them complete each sentence. Refer back to these Rules every time you use the Playbook. Repeating the rules helps reinforce what they are learning.
Comments/ Extra activities:	Explore other games they like to play (sports, board games, etc.) and ask them how the rules make winning the game possible. If you haven't done so already, by all means buy financial board games. Just check Amazon and you'll find many.
Vocabulary:	Principles, rules, energy, habits, invest, financial freedom, adventure, assets, liabilities.

HOW MONEY WORKS

Rules of The Money Game (Creative Wealth Principles). You have to know the rules in order to win the game.

1. Financial freedom is your _____.

2. You are the CEO of your life; financial _____ is your responsibility.

3. Your thoughts, _____ and attitudes determine your wealth potential.

4. Being _____ is a temporary financial condition, being _____ is a state of mind.

5. _____ it, _____ it, _____ it down.

6. Life is an adventure; let _____ be your guide.

7. To be financially successful, learn the _____ of money.

8. Money is a _____ to reach your dreams.

9. Money buys you stuff, not _____.

10. Make money grow by putting it to _____ for you.

11. Pay yourself _____.

12. To create financial freedom, _____ the energy of money wisely.

13. Most people don't _____ to fail, they fail to _____.

14. It's not how much money you make that's important, it's how much you _____.

15. If you can't afford it in _____, you can't afford it at all.

16. Save early, save _____.

17. Financial success comes from managing _____, not avoiding it.

18. Interest is only _____ when you're _____ it.

19. Don't put all your financial _____ into one basket.

20. Invest with your head, not with your _____.

21. Assets _____ you, liabilities _____ you.

22. It is better to tell your money where to _____ than to ask where it _____.

23. Only _____ money when it's going to _____ you money.

24. If you don't know where you're _____, any road will take you there.

25. Creating financial freedom is a matter of developing the right _____.

26. Make more money than you _____ and _____ less than you make.

27. Your money _____ always add up in the end.

28. Helping _____ is helping _____.

29. Leverage turns an ounce of _____ into a ton of _____.

30. _____ money creates an income; _____ money creates a life.

THE TRUTH ABOUT MILLIONAIRES

Principle/ Lesson:	Your thoughts, beliefs and attitudes influence your wealth potential. It's not how much money you make that's important, it's how much you keep. You can't tell how much money people have by looking at them or their lifestyle, The people we often 'think' look like wealthy people are often in debt and the people we often 'think' are poor often have a lot of money.
What:	Our thoughts are controlled to a large degree by the belief systems that we develop from infancy. We develop belief systems in three ways: from the things we see, from the things we hear and from the things we feel/experience emotionally through individual events that happen in our lives. We acquire beliefs from our parents, friends, society, culture, teachers, media. The money beliefs that we go into adulthood with are generally beliefs that were imparted on us by family, friends, media...everyone and everything we come into contact with and are exposed to as children. The challenge is that so many financial beliefs are incorrect and with incorrect beliefs come unsupportive money thoughts, choices and actions. In order to change these beliefs, you first have to understand and become aware that they exist and are driving you. You then must intentionally replace unsupportive beliefs with supportive ones.
Why:	You must understand that it's not just the act of making a lot of money that creates financially free people. They literally think differently about money and wealth and have different priorities and how they view life in regard to making, saving, investing and donating their financial resources (money).
How:	Read # 1-8 out loud with your child and talk about each one. Notice how you react to these statements as well and see if they conflict with your own thoughts, beliefs and attitudes.
Comments/ Extra activities:	The books, *The Millionaire Next Door and The Millionaire Woman Next Door*, by Robert Stanley, are books about millionaires that just may surprise you. If your child likes to read and is really interested, assign that book as extra reading.
Vocabulary:	Millionaire, frugal, self-sufficient, energy, wealth.

Millionaires are millionaires because they...

1. Spend less money than they make.

2. Buy assets (put their money to work for them).

3. Feel that Financial Freedom is more important than Social Status!

4. Spend their time, energy and money building wealth. In other words, they work at it and don't expect it to be given to them.

5. Live on their own without parents helping them financially.

6. Have own adult children are financially self-sufficient.

7. Are great at seeing business opportunities.

8. Chose the right occupation

Building wealth takes discipline, sacrifice and hard work!

What are the three words that describe the typical millionaire?

Frugal • Investors • Creators

Financially free people save money and invest in, and create assets, instead of spending their money on 'piddlyjunk' that decreases in value!

THE CHOICE IS YOURS!

YOUR MONEY BELIEFS	
Principle/ Lesson:	Your thoughts, beliefs and attitudes influence your wealth potential. Money only makes you more of what you already are.
What:	This page is designed to invite your child (and you) to explore what he thinks about money. You can teach anyone 'how' to make money, but without developing healthy thoughts, beliefs, and attitudes about money, he may have trouble keeping it.
Why:	Because your thoughts, beliefs and attitudes about money and wealth control your decisions and choices about your money, it's critical that you understand what's driving you at an unconscious level.
How:	Ask your child the first three questions and let him think about them and talk about them with you, or other kids. See if he can come up with beliefs in each of these three areas: himself, parents and friends. Then, have him finish the next two sentences. There are no right or wrong answers. Explore where he might have developed his beliefs about rich people and poor people. If you discover that you or your child believes that rich = greedy, selfish, mean, evil, or bad, discuss with them why believing this about rich people will often stop them, subconsciously, from becoming rich themselves. If you believe rich people are greedy, evil, or bad, and you don't want to become greedy, evil or bad, then why would you want to become rich? Lastly, fill in the blank on question #3.
Comments/ Extra activities:	Research "money belief systems" on the internet to find additional articles or activities. Do the activity yourself. You might be surprised at what you discover about your own money beliefs. Parents: A great book on financial beliefs is Secrets of the Millionaire Mind by T. Harv Eker.
Vocabulary:	Money, rich, poor.

YOUR MONEY BELIEFS

1. What do you think about money?

_____

_____

2. What do your parents say about money?

_____

_____

3. What do your friends say about money?

_____

_____

Finish the following sentences:

1. Rich people are....

_____

_____

2. Poor people are....

_____

_____

3. Most people think money means this:

_____

_____

F _ _ _ _ _ D _ M!

YOUR NEW A-B-Cs

Principle/ Lesson:	What you think about, you bring about. Human beings are creatures of habit.
What:	This page is designed to continue exploring the idea that our emotions are a result of what we think and that our thoughts are a result of all the things we do, all the choices we make, and all the situations we experience. As a result, our brains function on autopilot and the only way to change our behavior and our choices is to recognize that our beliefs, thoughts and attitudes are at the root of them.
Why:	Because our thoughts, beliefs and attitudes about money and wealth control our decisions and choices about our money, we need to understand how to change those thoughts, beliefs and attitudes so they are supportive of our goals and dreams.
How:	Have your child read through the information and walk him through the A-B-C process. Ask him what new habit he'd like to create and make a plan to put that new habit into practice for the next few months. While it used to be a common belief that it takes 21 days to make or break a habit, the latest studies don't support this. It depends on the person, the intensity of the habit, the type of habit, and mostly, whether the new habit will bring about something the person has set as a top priority. It's always more effective to start doing something positive than to try to stop doing something negative. Try to create habits that are supportive and will eventually override a nonsupportive habit.
Comments/ Extra activities:	Share with your child any situation where you have a habit that has been on autopilot and how you overcame a habit that wasn't good for you.
Vocabulary:	Neurons, synapses, consequence, belief, habit.

Our **Brains** are made up of **12 billion tiny cells** called **Neurons**. These neurons pass messages to each other (like passing notes in class) and create roads in our brains called **Synapses** to deliver those messages. One neuron is capable of forming as many as **50,000** synapses with other neurons creating a possible freeway system of more than **100 trillion synapses**.

When a road is created and used several times, a mental pattern develops. As we **see**, **hear**, **feel**, **smell**, **sense**, or **taste** something over and over again, our brains remember it. When we experience it, or something like it again, our brains activate the same chemical responses and existing thought patterns and we go on **cruise control or autopilot**. Being on cruise control can work **for** us or **against** us depending on whether it's a negative mental pattern or a positive mental pattern.

The A-B-C Game is a tool to change our thoughts. It helps us reprogram our brains (our mental computers) so we can make more supportive choices.

A = Action   B = Belief   C = Consequence

ACTIVITY:

Use your imagination to picture something new. Our minds can't tell the difference between imagination and reality. If we repeat this new pattern over and over again, for several months, it becomes a new highway and we begin to think differently and make better choices in our lives as a result.

How the A-B-C Game works...

A. Something happens to you or someone does something.

B. You **THINK** a certain thought because of a belief you have.

C. This thought makes you feel and make choices in a certain way.

"B" controls your behavior and choices, so by changing "B" your behavior and choices will change.

YOUR THOUGHTS, BELIEFS AND ATTITUDES

Principle/ Lesson:	Your thoughts, beliefs and attitudes influence your wealth potential. Human beings are meaning making machines.
What:	Assumptions are at the root of virtually every misunderstanding in life. We think a wrong thought about someone or something which leads to a wrong assumption. Wrong assumptions lead to all manner of discord in virtually every relationship you ever have...including the one you have with yourself!
Why:	Same as previous page.
How:	Walk through the example and then go through A, B, C. Do the exercise with your child so they can see how it applies to you as an adult also. Share with your child situations in your own life where you reacted poorly because of an assumption you made that was incorrect and how you felt as a result of assuming something.
Comments/ Extra Activities:	Use this page on an ongoing basis when you see your child (or yourself) have an emotional reaction to a situation where they made an assumption about someone or something that wasn't true. This will help set them up in the future for being in control of their emotions instead of blaming others for what they 'did' to them. It's all in what we make things "**mean**." **Note**: This is one of the MOST important LESSONS in our program and applies to every aspect of our lives. Because human beings are 'meaning making machines', the challenge is that we all too often ascribe incorrect meanings to things and that, in turn, causes us and others so much misery and heartache. The younger we learn that there isn't just one meaning to anything and the meaning we give things is what shapes our reality, the better the chances are, and the sooner, that we can create a life filled with love, health and happiness.
Vocabulary:	Response, meaning, assume.

EXAMPLE:

Event that happened - You don't get invited to a party.

Thought 1. "There must be something wrong with me, I'm stupid,"

Your response: Get mad or depressed, avoid people who went to the party. Think about ways to get back at them.

BUT...you could choose another thought based on a different belief OR based on the correct information, like maybe they just forgot to invite you or you didn't get the invitation in the mail for some reason.

Thought 2. "Something must have happened to the invitation or something else is going on that I just don't understand yet."

Your new response: Not a big deal, go on with life. It's just a party.

It ALL has to do with your 'core belief' about you and your friends.

YOUR TURN...Come up with your own A-B-C example: School, friends, sports, coach.

A. List something someone did/said recently that you got upset, mad or sad about...

_____

_____

B. What thoughts did you have and what did you make it mean? How do you know if those thoughts about what happened were really true?

_____

_____

C. What did you do because of the thing that happened? Can you figure out how your thoughts about it caused your behavior? Can you find the belief under the thought? How could you have thought about the situation differently.

_____

_____

Negative emotions happen most often when we make things mean something other than the truth, in other words, we ASSUME the wrong thing.

LEARN ABOUT YOUR MONEY ANIMAL	
Principle/ Lesson:	We're often hard-wired from birth to be a certain way with money but we can change. Knowing your money personality will help you understand your behavior in regard to money as a child and an adult.
What:	Everyone grows up fitting into one or more money personality styles. This is a simplified version but there are generally five main styles: hoarder, spender, monk, avoider and amasser.
Why:	It's important to have an awareness of your own money personality in order to begin to understand why you make the money choices you do. This helps you make changes in your behavior that will make it easier to reach your financial goals.
How:	Read the descriptions of each money personality and have your child circle the one he recognizes as his own. Tell him it's normal to be a combination of styles. See if he can recognize yours as well. Share how your style 'shows up' in your life and have a conversation about how each of the styles might look in adult behavior, especially how they might interact when different styles are married, work together, etc.
Comments/ Extra activities:	Have your child identify the different money personality styles in other family members and friends and even media personalities. **Note**: there are several additional personality styles. For more information, go to the web and search for 'money styles' or 'money personalities' and see what you can find. One of the personalities not mentioned here is the 'hoarder.' This person doesn't spend money on anything, lives frugally and refuses to share his money with anyone for any reason. This person lives in fear of losing his wealth, i.e., he has a scarcity mentality, not an abundance mentality. This is a great time to chat with your kids about abundance and scarcity. Have your child look up both terms in the dictionary and talk about each concept. This is a great time to discuss your beliefs with him as well.
Vocabulary:	Abundance, scarcity.
	Discover your money personality here: https://www.moneyharmony.com/moneyharmony-quiz and www.money-therapy.com is a great resource for information on the psychological aspects of money.

The Money Monk

She doesn't feel that money is worth her time or energy. Money is beneath her. She just can't be bothered.

The Saver

He likes to save up for things he wants to buy and for a rainy day in case he needs money for something.

The Avoider

She hates dealing with money. She avoids paying bills, looking at credit card statements or paying back debts.

The Spender

He spends every cent as soon as he gets it on piddlyjunk. He often spends more than he has and never has any saved.

SETTING GOALS – YOUR KEY TO SUCCESS

Principle/ Lesson:	If you don't know where you're going, any road will take you there. People don't get what they want when they don't know what they want.
What:	Goal setting is a very important step to accomplishing anything and to set goals, you have to have a clue about what you want to create or accomplish.
Why:	Studies have shown that the most significant difference between people who reach their goals and people who don't is that the people who reach their goals actually write their goals down and write, refine and modify them down often. Writing goals can be a scary process for someone who hasn't yet had much success in life because he may feel that the act of writing his goals down on paper is just another commitment he won't keep and hence, another failure in the making. Research doesn't back this up however.
How:	Ask your child to define the word GOAL. Talk about the difference between short-term goals (things you want to accomplish or create in less than a year) and long-term goals (things to accomplish or create that will take more than a year). Then, ask your child to come up with one short-term and one-long term goal. Follow that with the four questions about the goal. You can use both the short-term and long-term goal or have your child pick the one he wants to use.
Comments/ Extra activities:	Have your child go through goal setting in other areas of his life: school, sports, music, friends, health, etc. Plan a family vacation using a budget to figure costs for travel, distance, activities, food, etc. Discuss how important it is to plan and set goals in order to accomplish things. **IMPORTANT NOTE:** There are both goal-oriented people and process-oriented people. Goal setting for process-oriented people is painful and not productive and doesn't work for them. They are better at short-term projects than goals. A great book to read to understand this more is called **Goal-Free Living** by Stephen Shapiro is you suspect you or your child is process-oriented.
Vocabulary:	Goals, overcome, obstacle.

GOALS – YOUR KEY TO SUCCESS

A GOAL is something you want to achieve. It's good to have short-term and long-term goals. You can have a career goal, a financial goal, a sport or art goal, or any other thing you'd like to experience or accomplish.*

SHORT-TERM (one year or less)

(Example: I want to buy a new bike in 6 months)

Write a short-term goal here: _____

LONG-TERM (more than one year)

(Example: I want to save $5000 by the time I graduate from H.S.)

Write a long-term goal here: _____

QUESTIONS TO ASK ABOUT YOUR GOALS...

1. Why do you want this goal?

_____

2. What actions do you need to take to reach this goal?

_____

3. What might stand in your way?

_____

4. How might you overcome this obstacle?

_____

The biggest difference between people who **Reach Their Goals** and people don't is that they...

WRITE THEM DOWN REGULARLY!

GOAL SETTING

Principle/ Lesson:	A goal is dream with a deadline. A goal without a plan is just a wish.
What:	Without a well thought out plan, goals are hard to accomplish. Even if you don't know every step, having thought out the first few steps will propel you to the next steps.
Why:	If you never reach a goal, you'll stop having them. And if you stop having goals, you'll find it challenging to enjoy a meaningful life. Even if the goals you set are small, the simple act of working towards them gives our lives meaning and purpose.
How:	Use this sheet for additional goal setting.
Comments/ Extra activities:	RE: Process-oriented vs. Goal-oriented: As mentioned on the previous page, if your child is a process-oriented individual, it's critical that both you and he/she know this. It is a life-changer to understand. You see, if you are a process-oriented person (and this seems to be more common with females than males), the idea and activity of being asked to set goals makes them want to run and hide. They are often simply unable to do the activity because they don't think about the present and future like goal-oriented people do. They literally can't imagine setting one goal and then working towards it. They are more concerned and focused on what they are currently doing, creating an enjoyable environment for themselves, making sure what they are involved with is purposeful, fulfilling...things like that. Do not force a process-oriented person to do a lot of goal setting, however, please do explore with them with ideas of process-oriented vs. goal oriented and let them know there is nothing at all wrong with them. They simply see their lives, and the world, differently.
Vocabulary:	Short term goal, long term goal, obstacle.

GOAL SETTING

SHORT TERM GOAL:_____

1. Why do you want this goal?

_____

_____

2. What actions/steps do you need to take to reach this goal?

_____

_____

3. What might stand in your way?

_____

_____

4. How might you overcome this obstacle?

_____

_____

LONG TERM GOAL:_____

1. Why do you want this goal?

_____

_____

2. What actions/steps do you need to take to reach this goal?

_____

_____

3. What might stand in your way?

_____

_____

4. How might you overcome this obstacle?

_____

_____

THE POWER OF AFFIRMATIONS OR DECLARATIONS

Principle/ Lesson:	What you focus on expands. What you think about, you bring about. How you do anything is how you do everything.
What:	It's a fact that we are what we think about, and research has shown that our minds don't know the difference between imagination and reality. Your brain HEARS what you say about yourself and wants to make it true for you.
Why:	Human beings spend more time degrading themselves than speaking positively about themselves, both in their internal dialogue as well as speaking to others. Setting the stage for positive thinking will lead your child to success quicker than anything else.
How:	Explain Affirmations or Declarations are a way to verbalize what you want in life. You're affirming or declaring that they are already true. Go over the **Four P** requirements for positive affirmations/declarations: • personal • positive • present tense • practical Because your mind doesn't know the difference between imagination and reality, using affirmations is a great way to install positive self-talk as a way of reaching goals and creating life just the way they want it. Have your child come up with at least one affirmation/declaration in each category. Do the exercise along with your child to help illustrate how to do this. Here are some examples for each one: Money - I invest my money wisely every month. Health - I eat fruit every day. Friends - I have friends who listen and support my life. School - I do my homework every day. Family - I do something helpful for my parents every day. Stand up, put your hand on your chest and say the affirmations out loud.
Comments/ Extra activities:	An affirmation or declaration cannot have the word 'not' in it. In other words, you wouldn't say, "I don't eat candy all day." Weirdly enough, the brain doesn't actually register the negative words.
Vocabulary:	Affirmation, declaration.

The 4 P's of Positive Affirmations/Declarations

·1. BE PERSONAL. (USE I, ME, MY)

2. BE POSITIVE. (NOT I DON'T, BUT I DO)

3. USE THE PRESENT TENSE (ACT AS IF IT IS)

4. BE PRACTICAL.

Examples

I am healthy.
I save 10% of my income.
I am physically fit.
I am happy.

Come up with some affirmations/declaration of your own:

Money: _____

Health: _____

Friends: _____

School: _____

Family: _____

Other: _____

Other: _____

CREATING THE LIFE YOU WANT

Principle/ Lesson:	What you think about, you bring about. You are the *CEO* of your own life.
What:	The idea of being able to design and create the life you want is foreign to many adults. Most adults are still under the misunderstanding that life just happens to them, but science is beginning to show us otherwise. We are either at Cause or at Effect of life. Too often people grow up and become 'fire fighters' who react to life, rather than 'architects' who create the lives they want to live. There is a lot of research (see books below) that now show that the energy of our thoughts affect everything...even people and things we're thinking about that aren't in the same area. This information help kids begin to think and dream about life in a way that empowers them to create their lives instead of simply assuming that they have to deal with whatever happens to them.
Why:	The more adults who understand the concept of deliberate creation (aka manifestation) who take a proactive role in the design of their lives, the fewer adults there will be who rely on the 'system' to get by. This is a very good thing!
How:	Ask your child if they know anyone who has set out to create something specific in their life. Ask if they think this person spent time 'thinking' about what they wanted to create and have a conversation about it. If it has happened to your child this is a plus! Remember that the brain doesn't distinguish between imagination and reality. Talk to them about movies and ask what their favorite movies are and why. Introduce the idea of seeing what they want in their mind's eye as their own personal movie. Using one of their goals, have them write out a short mental movie of their future life. It's important for them to be as specific as possible. Example: don't write, I have a pet. Write, I have a German Shepard dog!
Comments/ Extra activities:	If applicable, share a time when you thought of someone and they called or you ran into them, or you kept visualizing something you wanted or needed and it just appeared. Isn't life fun when this happens? Books: Read anything by Joe Dispenza, Dawson Church, Lynne McTaggart or Bruce Lipton just to name a few. Also, sit down and watch the movie The Secret with your child/children.
Vocabulary:	Deliberate creation, manifestation, cause, effect.

CREATING THE LIFE YOU WANT

Deliberate Creation (aka Manifestation):

The process of creating what we want in life. Most people don't GET what they want because they don't KNOW what they want!

How to begin to manifest what you want:

• Think about your goals and what's important to you and then write them down.

• Create positive thoughts, feelings, and emotion, pictures and words about it.

• Let those images attract the reality into your life.

NOW...Write out YOUR Mental Movie:

If you were to write a short movie about how you want your life to be, what would that movie look like? What would the movie be called?

_____

_____

_____

_____

_____

_____

_____

You have to be able to SEE and FEEL what you want first!

What you THINK about, you BRING about!

BE, DO, HAVE	
Principle/ Lesson:	Be the person you want to be right now! Financial freedom is your choice.
What:	Be Do Have is a philosophical way of thinking and behaving that attracts what you want into your life.
Why:	If you ask a group of adults what comes first, Being, Doing or Having, most people get this backwards. They think they have to HAVE something before they can DO something and then they'll be able to BE a certain way. It actually works the other way around. In order to HAVE what you want in life, you first have to BE that way which then leads to you DOING the things that then allow you to HAVE what you want in life.
How:	Walk through the words with your child, using an example of your own. A very common myth is when people think they have to lose weight in order to do the things that then make them happy when in reality, if they choose to be happy, they will do the things naturally that lead them to choose the right foods, exercise and be the right weight. For adults, this also is a very common misconception in regard to relationships. People think they have to have the right relationship in order to be happy when in actuality, if they choose to be happy first, they will much more easily find the right relationship. Explore with your child things they think they have to have in order to be happy, popular, smart, etc., and then talk about how they could be happy, satisfied, etc., first.
Comments/ Extra activities:	Have your child take three pieces of paper and write in big bold letters, BE on one, DO on another and HAVE on the third. Arrange them HAVE, DO, and BE at first and explain that this is how most people do things. Have them guess at how it really works. Surprisingly, the kids in our summer camp programs usually figure this out faster than adults!
Vocabulary:	Being, doing, having.

HAVE

↓

DO

↓

BE

Many people think that they have to **HAVE** something (like a big house, fancy car, perfect body), in order to be able to **DO** what they really want, and this will then allow them to **BE** happy (or popular or creative or at peace or...).

BE

↓

DO

↓

HAVE

In reality, it works the other way around.

Life works much easier when we focus on **BEING** a certain way first (being creative, being happy, being healthy, being satisfied, being kind, etc.).

When we're **BEING** a certain way, we then naturally **DO** the things that allow us to **HAVE** the things we want, will enjoy and feel proud of.

Name something you thought you had to **HAVE** in order to **DO** something to **BE** a certain way? _____

_____

_____

CREATING DREAM BOARDS	
Principle/ Lesson:	What you focus on expands. What you think about, you bring about. Thoughts are things.
What:	A Dream Board is a visually creative way to illustrate the dreams, desires and goals you want to draw into your life. Before anything is created outwardly in the world, it is first a thought in someone's head.
Why:	As we've mentioned, our brains don't know the difference between imagination and reality, and the biggest difference between people who successfully create what they want in life and those who don't is the process of repeatedly writing down what they want. Creating a Dream Board is a fun and highly effective way to visualize on paper what you want to create in your life.
How:	Get a piece of poster board, stickers, colored pens, pencils, crayons, magazines, photos of items your child has a passion for already (sports, horses, playing a musical instrument, etc.), and have him create a physical representation of the things that interest him. Ask your child the following questions: 1) What kind of place might they like to live? City? Country? Island? 2) What type of activities do they want to be participating in? 3) What types of people do they enjoy? Do they want pets? 4) Anything else that will spark their imagination for their future.
Comments/ Extra activities:	Dream boards are a great family activity as well. Create a new ritual of making new dream boards on January 1 of each year. You can create a family dream board as well as individual boards for each family member. Most families don't sit down and create family goals (vacations, where they want to live, experiences they'd like to have together, etc.). This is a great opportunity for everyone to learn the power of a Dream Board (and it IS very powerful). Even if you yourself don't believe it, try it and see! If nothing more, it's a great opportunity to be creative and creativity in life has all sorts of positive benefits. For a great app, check out www.MindMovies.com!
Vocabulary:	Dream board, goals.

Building Your Dream Board

This is your chance to put on paper what you 'see' in your future. Use the examples below to give you some ideas of what you may want to include on your Dream Board.

Career?

Car?

Who do you want to be?

Sports?

Friends?

Hobbies?

House?

What type of person do you want to be?

How do you want to feel?

Travel?

Pets?

How do you want to spend your days?

Stuff?

THIS STUFF CALLED MONEY

Principle/ Lesson:	Money is a tool to reach your dreams. Money is energy.
What:	Everyone has different ideas of what the words money, value, wealth and rich mean. We want to begin to instill the idea that money is simply energy and a means to an end, not the end in itself. It's a tool. The term 'value' is relative. It relates to how precious something is to someone. One person may 'value' a thing more than another person and that's perfectly OK. This is why some things go up in value and other things don't. The term 'wealth' is subjective but normally refers to the amount of 'value' in a person's life. Wealth can relate to money, friends, family, love, etc. You can have a wealth of knowledge, a wealth of friends, etc. The term 'rich' is generally used to describe someone who has a lot of wealth. The key is to be able to use the words without emotions or judgments attached to them. It's the judgments that get us into emotional upheaval.
Why:	Since everyone has a different definition in his mind for these words, it's great to explore them with your child.
How:	Have your child take a few minutes to finish the sentences and then explore with him the terms as we explained them above. Share your own ideas of what these terms mean as well.
Comments/ Extra activities:	It's a great idea to do this activity with your whole family. Often we develop beliefs about what things mean unconsciously so by exploring them consciously, you can develop an awareness of how your beliefs about what these terms mean may be affecting your own decisions about money and creating wealth. Look up foreign currency rates on the internet and talk about how different countries' money is 'worth' different amounts of our money; how a vacation can be expensive in another country where the US dollar is undervalued and less expensive in a country where the dollar is over valued. Visit this great site to explore what the US dollar is worth in different currencies: www.xe.com/ucc. Explore the "History of Money" on the web and discuss with your child.
Vocabulary:	Money, value, wealth, rich.

Finish these sentences.

Money is...

_____

_____

_____

Value is...

_____

_____

_____

Wealth is...

_____

_____

_____

Rich is...

_____

_____

_____

WHAT'S IT WORTH	
Principle/ Lesson:	What something is worth depends on who is valuing it and what they're using it for. Supply and demand plays a large role in how things are valued.
What:	Different things are valuable to different people. Some people value money while others value cows. There are advantages and disadvantages to the different 'things' we think are valuable.
Why:	To be able to evaluate the advantages and disadvantages of different types of assets that your child can acquire that can lead to financial freedom as an adult.
How:	Ask your child to come up with as many advantages and disadvantages as they can for the six items on this page. Here are some ideas...

Cash: convenient, easy to break into small pieces, light weight, universally accepted; but it's not safe to carry large amounts of cash, can't transport it easily to other countries, different types of currency all over the world.

Gold, silver: standard in the world representing a certain value, good to have in case of devaluation of currencies (paper money); inconvenient to carry around (heavy), value goes up and down with world's economies, hard to split up to buy/trade for small things.

Jewels: beautiful, can wear them, their value is often maintained over long periods of time; can be stolen for its value, can get lost out of its jewelry setting.

Livestock: can multiply, can feed you meat and milk; can get sick and die, hard to exchange for something smaller and of less value, difficult to carry around.

Real estate: usually goes up in value over long periods of time, can get a loan to purchase it, hard to destroy, you can live on it, rent it out; it can go down in value, it can burn down or get destroyed, it can be a lot of work and maintenance can be expensive.

Idea: there is an unlimited supply of great ideas in the world that can do good and make you money; people spend a lot of time, energy and money trying to make some ideas valuable but don't succeed. |
| **Comments/ Extra activities:** | Come up with additional things that human beings might value and be able to exchange with each other. Talk about why some people value some things and some people value others.

Have your child look up 'bartering' and do a little report on how it started, why it was made illegal in the 1930s (government couldn't tax it), how it's still done today as organizations, etc. |
| **Vocabulary:** | Currency, gold, silver, jewels, real estate, livestock, ideas, advantage, disadvantage. |
| | |

	Advantages	Disadvantages
	_____	_____
	_____	_____
	_____	_____
	_____	_____
	_____	_____
	_____	_____
	_____	_____
	_____	_____
	_____	_____
	_____	_____
	_____	_____
	_____	_____
	_____	_____
	_____	_____
	_____	_____
	_____	_____
	_____	_____
	_____	_____

THE POWER OF A DOLLAR

Principle/ Lesson:	Money makes the world go round! Economics is the study of how money circulates in the world.
What:	How money circulates is the basis for all understanding of both micro and macro economics, i.e., how the world's economies function. A basic understanding of the limitlessness of what one dollar can buy over and over again begins to instill the concept of abundance, that there's plenty of money and wealth for everyone.
Why:	Often, adults who can't seem to create financial freedom function from a scarcity mentality; that there's not enough money (or food or jobs or houses or opportunities, etc.) to go around. They think that everyone else already has what's available so why bother. Having an abundance mentality allows your child to understand that there's plenty of wealth in the world for everyone, including them. It allows them to have big dreams about life and what they can create for themselves and others. NOTE: when we talk about abundance we're talking about the unlimited source of wealth that can be created with ideas, business, etc. We are not referring to the world's physical resources which are limited and should be conserved and used wisely.
How:	This activity can be done with a large number of people so if you can do it with your family members or at a gathering, all the better. Otherwise, simply go over the page by reading around the circle to see how money circulates and then talk about how fear affects how our economy speeds up or slows down.
Comments/ Extra activities:	With a large group of people: Stand in a circle with one person starting with a one dollar bill. Have that person state how they get money and name something they'd spend this dollar on (e.g., "I own a movie theater and I'm going to buy popcorn for my snack shop."). The next person takes on the role of whoever the last person bought something from, (e.g., "I own a business that sells snacks to movie theaters and I need to buy a computer to run my business."). Each person carries this on until they reach the end of the circle (the first person who had the dollar). Everyone can now see how the same dollar bill can buy an unlimited number of things in the world! Look up the term 'zero-sum game' and have a conversation with this concept with your child.
Vocabulary:	Money circulation, economy, infinite, scarcity, abundance.

You buy shampoo from the store. The store pays a vendor for bags. The bag company pays a vendor to print its logo on the bags. The printing company pays an employee. The employee goes out to dinner. The restaurant buys onions at the market and on and on!

Start Here!

Our economy speeds up or slows down because of how people are spending (circulating) their money. If they hold on to it and don't spend, the economy slows down. If they spend it quickly, the economy speeds up.

Paper money circulates until it wears, out but the amount of 'value' in the world is infinite! Anyone can come up with an idea that can create infinite wealth and make a huge difference in the world.

THE TWO TYPES OF INCOME

Principle/ Lesson:	Earning money and making money are different. Making money is more fun! Passive income is the key to financial freedom.
What:	Income is classified in two main categories: earning and making. You EARN money when you trade your time and energy for money; you MAKE money by investing your time, energy and money in assets that produce passive income in some way (rental income, business profits, stock dividends). The way to know the difference is to look at how many times you get paid for every hour you work. If you get paid once for every hour you work, this is Earned Income, as an example, if you are paid by the hour at a job. If you get paid more than once for every hour you work, this is Making money or Passive Income. An example of this is if you were to write a book and get a royalty every time someone bought a copy. BIG NOTE: Passive income rarely means that it takes no work at all...it just means you're not trading every hour of work for an hourly wage.
Why:	Knowing what kind of income comes you're bringing into your life helps you make wiser career and investment decisions. If you never create passive income sources for yourself, you will always be trading your time and energy for money and it's very difficult to retire (not work) at some point in your life because social security paychecks will never be enough to live on (nor where they meant to be).
How:	Simply go over the following page, asking your child to come up with examples of each type of income if they can. Help them as needed. NOTE: Portfolio income is always passive income but passive income is not always portfolio income.
Comments/ Extra activities:	Have your child ask family and friend's parents about the different types of income they create and how they create it. Remember, if you have an issue with this, it's because you make money 'mean' more than it really is. Let your child be innocent and learn from other's decisions and choices. Also, you can prep the person your child wants to talk to so they know they will be asking about this. For more information, please read Robert Kiyosaki's two great books, *Rich Dad, Poor Dad* and *Cash Flow Quadrant*.
Vocabulary:	Earned income, passive income, profit, rental income, dividends, royalties.

THE TWO TYPES OF INCOME

EARNING MONEY = EARNED INCOME

Money you EARN by trading your time and energy for:

- As an employee in a job
- When you're self-employed and own a job...in other words, you don't get paid unless YOU are doing the work...example: plumber, graphic artist, landscaper.

MAKING MONEY = PASSIVE INCOME

Money you MAKE from investing in:

- a business (profit) - brick & mortar store or online
- real estate (rental income, loaning money to others to buy)
- The stock market (dividends)

In order to tell if your income is Earned or Passive, just look at how many times you get paid for every hour you work.

If you only get paid once for every hour you work, you are EARNING money.

If you get paid more than once for every hour you work, you are MAKING money.

FINANCIAL FOURSQUARE

Principle/ Lesson:	I choose how to earn and make my money. Everyone needs to be an Investor.
What:	There are four primary ways of looking at the ways people earn and make their money: as an employee, as a self-employed person, as a business owner (with employees who make you money using leverage) and as an investor.
Why:	People often don't consider the income and other ramifications (control, responsibility, taxes, income limitations) when choosing careers or what jobs they might like to do. Financial foursquare is a way of looking at these choices with a different paradigm.
How:	For each square, explore the answers to the following questions: 1. Who hires you? 2. How are you paid (hourly, salary, commission, interest, appreciation)? 3. When and how much do you work (full-time, part-time, 9-5, weekends, nights, etc.)? 4. What skills, knowledge and other talents do you need? 5. What are your responsibilities? 6. Who puts money into (pays for) your retirement account? 7. Who takes the most risks? 8. Who pays your medical insurance? 9. Who controls how much money you can make/earn? 10. Can you deduct job expenses from your taxes? 11. Who controls your vacation time, time off, sick time? 12. What type of income are you creating (earned, passive)?
Comments/ Extra activities:	Regardless of which square you earn or make your money in, it's everyone's responsibility to learn how to be a Smart Investor because if YOU don't take care of your money, how is IT going to take care of you when you need it to sometime in the future.
Vocabulary:	Employee, self-employed, business owner, investor, earning money, making money.

FINANCIAL FOURSQUARE

Employee (95% of USA)

The Boss

You are trading your time and energy for money.

25-35 years to be a millionaire

Business Owner

Your employees time and energy making you money!

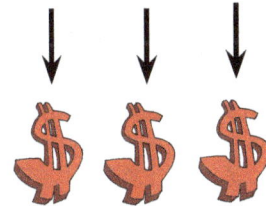

TEAMWORK!

10-15 years to be a millionaire

Earning Money

Making Money

Self-Employed (own a job)

You are now the boss but now you OWN a job and you're still trading your time and energy for money.

15-20 years to be a millionaire

Investor

Your money making money!

Can become financially free quickly

This concept is taken from "Rich Dad, Poor Dad" by Robert Kiyosaki

NOTE: there is NO wrong place to start.
The right/best way to earn or make money is the way that gives you joy and a sense of purpose and satisfaction!

FINANCIAL FOURSQUARE (continued)	
Principle/ Lesson:	I choose how I earn and make my money.
What:	Different types of jobs or career choices create different types of income.
Why:	When making choices in life with regard to creating financial freedom for yourself, it's important to understand how different types of income are created. Passive Income is the key to financial freedom so we want your child to understand what types of choices in terms of a job or career might create passive income faster or easier than others. Knowledge is power!
How:	Have your child go through each occupation and figure out which square from the previous activity the occupation fits into, keeping in mind that sometimes it could be more than one. For example, you may be employed by a school to be a teacher (employee) OR you may own a business where people hire you to teach (self-employed) OR you might own a company and have five teachers on staff who go out and teach for you and get a percentage of what you charge the client (business owner). Feel free to make a square on a piece of paper and write the occupations or jobs in the squares they fit in.
Comments/ Extra activities:	Have your child identify in which square family members might be placed. If your child has a job or career that they are already talking about or passionate about, have them identify in which square they will be working.
Vocabulary:	Occupation and many of the job/career titles may be new.

FINANCIAL FOURSQUARE

OCCUPATION	E	S	B	I	OCCUPATION	E	S	B	I
Teacher	E				Graphic Designer	E	S	B	
Financial Advisor	E	S			Attorney	E	S	B	
Receptionist	E				Bookkeeper	E			
Engineer	E				Day Trader				I
Waitress	E				Assembly worker	E			
Salesperson	E	S			Staff Accountant	E			
Landscape designer	E	S	B		Hair stylist	E	S	B	
Doctor	E				Shipping Clerk	E			
Software Company C.E.O.	E		B		Rock band drummer	E			
Psychiatrist	E	S	B		Real Estate Salesperson	E			
Car Repair Shop Owner			B		Maintenance	E			
Movie director	E				Administrative Assistant	E			
Researcher	E				Home Owner				I
Sony Electronics Owner			B		Amusement Park Owner			B	
Interior Decorator	E	S	B		Smoothie Store Operator	E			
Mayor	E				Supermarket Owner			B	
Real Estate Developer	E	S	B	I	Toy Inventor	E			
Software Engineer	E				Oprah Winfrey			B	
Restaurant Owner			B		Weather Man/Woman	E			
Garbage Man/Woman	E				Nurse	E			
House Painter	E	S	B		Electrician	E	S	B	

E = Employee; S = Self-employed; B = Business Owner; I = Investor

WHAT'S YOUR PASSION - DOING WHAT YOU LOVE

Principle/ Lesson:	Life's an adventure, let passion be your guide. Find a job you love and never have to 'work' another day in your life.
What:	Thinking about different careers which you are interested in BEFORE you go into them can sometimes save you a lot of time and money.
Why:	Your child now has a way of evaluating his career choices. We want all children to know that it's OK not to know what they want to do when they get to be adults...heck, most adults STILL don't know what they want to do when they grow up. Children should also know that it's OK to change jobs and careers if and when they figure out that they made a choice that wasn't exactly the best for them or simply want a new challenge or skill. Too many adults stay in jobs they dislike. It's a waste of your precious time and your life to stay in a career that makes you miserable. We live in a country where we can choice to do just about anything but kids need to know that anything is possible! If you are a parent who believes your child should get a good paying job with benefits so they are secure, nothing could be further from the truth. They will create security for themselves when they find out what they really want to do to contribute to the world and can get paid for the privileged of doing so. THIS is when life is truly an adventure worth living.
How:	Walk through the page and simply ask the questions and explore the answers. This is a great way to get your child thinking about the future and can often turn up some really interesting areas of interest.
Comments/ Extra activities:	Use your own life as examples. Americans, on average, have at least 7 different careers during their lifetimes and with more and more people turning to jobs involving technology, and jobs they can do from home or even when they are traveling, that number is going to increase.
Vocabulary:	Passion, occupation, career, potential, obsolete.

WHAT'S YOUR PASSION

Name an occupation or career you think you might like to try when you 'grow up'? _____

Now answer the following questions about that choice.

1) What is it about this occupation or career that's interesting to you?

_____

2) What type of education will you need?

_____

3) What skills will you need?

_____

4) What is the earning potential?

_____

5) Can you see this job becoming obsolete in the future?

_____

It's good to ask yourself these questions when you're looking at different jobs and careers. Most Americans have several careers (average is 7) during their lifetime. It's OK to not know what you want to do when you grow up. Some people never do!

There's no such thing as the greatest job. The best job for you is the one you enjoy doing!

WHERE DID ALL MY MONEY GO?	
Principle/ Lesson:	Employees generally pay more taxes than self-employed, business owners and investors. Awareness and knowledge are the first steps toward making informed choices.
What:	It's important to understand how to read a paycheck.
Why:	Most kids never see their parent's paycheck so the first time they get paid they are usually in shock when they see what their Net Income is (gross income minus taxes = net income). Learning about taxes and deductions prepares kids for understanding their first paycheck and know exactly what is being taken out and why.
How:	Go through the sample paycheck and help them answer the questions below the paycheck. Explain the terms Gross Income (hourly wage x hours worked) and Net Income (gross income - all of the taxes and deductions). Explain the different types of taxes. • Social security - federal government funded retirement supplement (employees and employers both contribute to this). • Medicare - federal health insurance that pays for a large portion of health care expenses for when you're over 65. • Federal Income Tax - military, social security, medicare, interest on federal government debt, security issues, government employees (and their retirements), environmental agencies, national parks, federal prisons, and more. • State Income Tax - not all states have state income taxes. State income taxes pay for state police, infrastructure like water and power plants, state parks, higher education (lower education is generally funded by local governments and property taxes), and more.
Comments/ Extra activities:	Show your child a copy of your paycheck and pay stub and answer the same questions.
Vocabulary:	Paycheck, gross income, net income, overtime, pay period, social security, federal tax, state taxes, medicare, deductions.

Sally's Shell Shop

Employee: John Smith
SSN: 123-12-1234
Pay Period: 6/1/06-6/15/06
Pay Date: 6/21/06
Net Pay: $231.71
Check No: 006022

HOURS			EARNINGS				
	Regular	O/T	Regular	Overtime	Bonus	Other	Gross Pay
T/P	40		$1,500.00		----	----	$1,500.00
YTD			$16,500				$16,500.00

DEDUCTIONS							
	Social Security Tax	Medicare Tax	Federal W/H Tax	State W/H Tax	Pension	Other	Net Pay
T/P	$85.85	$20.08	$198.85	$63.52	--	---	$1,016.32
YTD	$944.35	$220.88	$2187.35	$698.72	---	---	$11,179.52

O/T = Overtime, T/P = This period, YTD = Year to Date

1. Who is John's Employer? _____
2. How long is the pay period? _____
3. How many hours did he work? _____
4. How much does he get paid per hour? _____
5. How much does he get paid for overtime? _____
6. What was John's Gross Income? _____
7. What was John's Net Income? _____
8. How much Federal Tax did he pay? _____
9. What is John's Net Income YTD? _____
10. Do you want John's Job? _____

Remember, when you work for someone else (trade your time for money for money), you're earning money and you pay taxes first!

When you're self-employed, own a business or an investor, you pay taxes after deducting all your expenses from your income!

"No matter how rich you become, how famous or powerful, when you die the size of your funeral will still pretty much depend on the weather."
- Michael Pritchard

THE MONEY JARS – YOUR MAGICAL MONEY MANAGEMENT SYSTEM!

Principle/ Lesson:	People don't plan to fail, they fail to plan. Pay yourself first. It's better to tell your money where to go than to ask it where it went. It's not how much money you make that's important, it's how much you keep. Creating financial freedom is simply a matter of developing the right habits.
What:	The Money Jars is a simple but highly effective way to allocate one's income into categories that relate to real life. It's great to think of your money as having lots of jobs instead of one...spending.
Why:	Because human beings are creatures of habit, having children learn this simple money management habit teaches them effective money management skills early on in life. This is a great step towards creating financial freedom later in life.
How:	Use the verbiage on the next page to explain The Money Jars system to your child.
Comments/ Extra activities:	Have your child create his own set of jars. Be sure to use see-through glass or plastic so your child can see a visual accumulation of money in the jars. Parent challenge: Set up your own set of jars (or better yet, bank accounts with labels). NOTE: it is not usually a lack of money that's the problem for most people; it's an inability or unwillingness to manage the money they have. The Money Jars is a great way to help establish positive habits to work toward financial freedom. When explaining the Freedom jar, you can tell the story of the Golden Goose if your child doesn't already know it and if they do, revisit the story and moral. The story is included Note: For more detailed information, read through the Money Jars e-book that came along with this program, , go to our website and click on the store.
Vocabulary:	Habit, abundance, expenses, savings, donation, freedom, education, play.

THE MONEY JARS – YOUR MAGICAL MONEY MANAGEMENT SYSTEM

Your money has several different jobs. Three out of every four Americans live month to month which means they spend all of the money they make every month and don't save any money at all. In addition, many Americans actually spend MORE money than they make using credit cards. This is not the way to become financially free!

The first jar is for your *Living Expenses*...it's for things you NEED to live each month.

The second jar is your *Freedom Jar*. This is the money you INVEST regularly so it grows into more for your future. Think of this jar as your Golden Goose; every year it's needs to produce enough income (eggs) for you to live on when you stop working. *This is the most important jar of all because this is the money you to use to make you more money.*

The third jar is your *Savings Jar*. This jar is for your contingency money (also called your rainy day money or emergency fund). Imagine having SIX months worth of living expenses put away 'just in case'. As an example, if you lost your job, you could take more time to think about what you wanted to do next instead of having to scramble, looking for an new job as quickly as possible. This jar is also a place for you to save up for larger purchases. You can divide this jar into several smaller jars depending on what you're saving up for.

The fourth jar is your *Education Jar*. Wouldn't it be great if you had money saved up to continue your education once you're out of school? For kids, this jar is money can be for college or lessons. Most adults, once they are done with high school and maybe college, still want to take classes or go to seminars or workshops to learn about all sorts of things. This way you always have money to learn new things.

The fifth jar is your *Play Jar*, and it may be your favorite. This jar is for doing anything you wish that makes you happy and brings you pleasure. Lots of people work hard but never take time to play or spend their money for pleasure without feeling guilty about it. Your Play Jar gives you a way to always have money to spend any way you wish, and best of all, it's *guilt-free*. After all, most of us work hard for our money so we should be able to enjoy spending some of it on whatever we wish. It's all about balance.

The sixth jar is your *Giving or Donation Jar*. What if you believed there wasn't enough money in the world for everyone? Do you think you would feel comfortable donating a portion of your money to help others? Probably not. But if you believed there was an abundance or never-ending supply of wealth in the world, you'd probably feel great about giving some of your money, time or energy to others. Donating is a wealthy habit and we want you to practice it every day.

There is a Universal Law that works like this: if you give something away, it comes back to you multiplied. Don't ask us why, it just works that way and it has to do with your belief about abundance. Think of this in terms of doing something nice for someone or even simply smiling at a stranger or complimenting someone's appearance. That positive energy gets transferred to that other person, and then keeps getting transferred to others until it's finally returned back to you in some other form.

Q. What do we do if your child already has a savings account, checking account or other investment account?

A. Use the savings account as the Savings Jar and on a monthly basis, when your child gets his bank statement, write the balance on a piece of paper and put the paper in the jar. You can also keep track on a spread sheet on the computer. Use a checking account for the Living Expenses Jar. Use an investment account in conjunction with their Freedom Jar and every time your child has saved up the minimum amount to add to their investment account, transfer the money from their jar to the account.

Note: This is generally for older kids who have figured out a way to earn/make money already. You can also apply this if you're utilizing The Ultimate Allowance System.

Q. How did you come up with the percentages on the jars?

A. The percentages listed on the jars are for adults so explain this in terms of how an adult might divide up their income. (Remember, we're not raising kids...we're raising and training adults!)

Living - 55% (basic needs)

Freedom - $10% (long-term but maybe sooner)

Saving - 10% (just in case situations and short-term wants)

Education - 10% (continued education is vital for growth)

Play - 10% (wants right now)

Donation - 5% (practicing abundance is an important wealthy habit)

These percentages are only a guide, so you and your child can talk about how much of each dollar they earn/make they think should go into each jar. The key is to be consistent and develop the habit early on.

PARENT'S CHALLENGE: Set up your own set of jars and follow the program to set an example for your child. You may be surprised at what happens. Jars can be individual bank accounts or spread sheets keeping track of what money is in each 'jar account'.

Note: For more information on The Money Jars, read The Money Jars e-book and Secrets of the Millionaire Mind by T. Harv Eker or visit www.creativewealthintl.org/moneyjars.php

DO THE MONEY JARS!

All Your Income

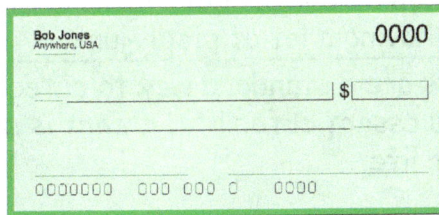

Bob Jones
Anywhere, USA

0000

$

0000000   000 000 0   0000

55%	10%	10%	10%	10%	5%

Living Expenses (needs & wants)

Financial Freedom Account

Savings: Contingency Vacation, etc.

Education

Play – Yeah!

Donations

YOUR MONEY'S MANY ROLES

Living
This money is for the money you need to live each month.

It includes your necessary household expenses and the things you think you really can't live without.

Freedom
This money is used to invest in ASSETS (stocks, rental property, business, etc.) that will produce PASSIVE INCOME for you to live on whenever you want.

Saving
This money is used as your Contingency Fund (rainy day money) and to make large purchases such as a house, car, college education, clothing, bike, vacations, computers, etc.

Education
This money is used for education, whether to pay for grad school, seminars or golf lessons.

It's important to keep learning!

Play
This money is used to do anything you wish with. Movies, massage, dinner out, candles... whatever you WANT.

You must spend this money every month!

Donating
This money is used to help others or the earth any way you wish.

By helping others you believe there is an abundant supply of money (energy) in the world, in other words, enough for everyone.

WANTS VS. NEEDS	
Principle/ Lesson:	Financially free people prioritize their spending into Needs vs. Wants. Financial free people believe that Financial Freedom is more important than status and having a lot of piddlyjunk.
What:	Needs and wants are a standard way to categorize expenses. A need is something that's essential for life; a want is something you desire that is not essential for life. Most wants have an emotional aspect to them in that we 'want' them because of how we think that thing is going to make us feel.
Why:	In order to evaluate whether or not you should spend your valuable financial resources (your money) on something, it's important to understand why you're making the choice you are making to spend money on a particular need or want.
How:	Have your child come up with different needs and wants and fill in the blanks on the next page. Then ask your child to think about how a child's needs and wants are different than an adult's. Also, explore how your child's 'wants' don't fit into your (parent's) list of needs and wants for the whole family. Piddlyjunk is the word we use for all the 'stuff' we waste our money on. Read the definition on the next page and list items. Spending our money on piddlyjunk isn't good or bad...it is simply choices we make that have financial consequences. We want your child to begin to think in terms of, "If I choose to save this money and invest it for later, it would be worth X but if I choose to spend it on piddlyjunk, it is gone forever."
Comments/ Extra activities:	Have your child go through your entire home and make a list of all of the 'stuff' that is in the house that no one uses very much or not at all. Discuss why these things were purchased in the first place (e.g., someone really had to have it, someone thought they would use it all of the time). Come up with the purchase prices for the list of things, add it up and write that figure here _____. (Prepare to be stunned.) Later, when we explore how money multiples, you can use this figure to compute how much it could be worth if the money had been invested (put to work) instead. Check out our **Needs vs. Wants Debate** we use in Camp Millionaire.
Vocabulary:	Wants, needs, piddlyjunk, financial consequences.

NEEDS VS. WANTS

NEEDS are things that are necessary for everyday life.

WANTS are things that bring us comfort or things that we'd like to have or do.

List several wants and needs that you have right now.

NEEDS	WANTS

List a few wants and needs you might have as an **adult**.

NEEDS	WANTS

Piddlyjunk: a **want** that either has NO value after you buy it (e.g., coffee drinks, lunch out every day, movie, etc.) OR loses value over time (e.g., music CDs, videos, sports equipment, cars, etc.). List the last 5 pieces of piddlyjunk that you have wasted financial energy on lately:

_____

_____

_____

YOUR MONEY JOURNAL

Principle/ Lesson:	Awareness is the first key to any change. If you always do what you've always done, you'll always get what you've always gotten! It's better to tell your money where to go instead of asking it where it went.
What:	Quite often, our desire to buy something (spend money) is tied to an emotional experience or feeling we anticipate from the 'thing' we're buying (e.g., fancy new car = excitement, feeling special; new clothes = feeling pretty, feeling rich or special, etc.). If we aren't aware of WHY we're making certain financial choices over and over again (spending habits), it's impossible to know what we need to change in order to experience a different result.
Why:	In order to reach financial freedom at some point in life, we have to make conscious choices with our money and in order to do that, we have to know what we're doing with the money that is running through our fingers. Getting kids to begin to think in terms of WHY they want to buy things is a great first step in helping them make wise spending and saving choices with their money.
How:	Ask your child to keep a log for a few days or even weeks of all the ways money comes into their lives and goes out of their lives. Review the difference between INCOME and EXPENSES and have them put the total amounts in the correct columns. Then ask your child to think about the 'why' underneath the purchase. Feel free to get your child a small journal or notebook to keep track of their money in.
Comments/ Extra activities:	Do this activity along with your child so they can see all the money that goes through your hands as well. You may be incredibly surprised at the amount of money you waste yourself and WHY you buy things.
Vocabulary:	Feelings, journal, awareness.

YOUR MONEY JOURNAL

Awareness is the first step in developing good money habits. Knowing where and why you spend your money helps you be in control of your financial future!

Date	Description/Feeling	Income?	Expense?
		Totals	

"Tell your money where to go instead of wondering where it went." by C. E. Hoover

Knowing where your money goes and where you're wasting your financial energy is the first step toward being in control of your financial future!

Teacher: If you had one dollar and you asked your father for another, how many dollars would you have?

Vincent: One dollar.

Teacher: You don't know your arithmetic.

Vincent: You don't know my father!

Q. Why did the man put his money in the freezer?

A. Because he wanted cold hard cash!

SPENDING AND SAVING PLAN - SSP (AKA A BUDGET)

Principle/ Lesson:	Most people don't plan to fail, they fail to plan. It's better to tell your money where to go than ask it where it went.
What:	A Spending and Savings Plan (SSP) is a powerful tool to help you reach your dreams.
Why:	Most adults view a budget like a diet, as something that limits or restricts them instead of a powerful tool to help them plan for their future. By showing kids how to use an SSP to plan for all types of events that may happen in their lives: future purchases, college, buying cars and houses, getting married, planning for kid's colleges, vacations, etc., you give them a tool to use for the rest of their lives.
How:	Read through the scenario on the next page. Have them put $3000 in the line across from Gross Income, $960 for taxes (review taxes and what they're used for) and finally $2040 for Net Income. Your child should be familiar with these terms from the Paycheck activity. Now have the kids divide the Net Income amount ($2040) into the jar percentages (adult version). Before leaving this preliminary page, go over the expenses on the bottom so they see all the 'little' expenses that pop up all the time. Feel free to add some of your own. Notice that they now have to see if they can live on $1122 as an adult. Let them know, however, that as a child or when they in college or just getting their first job, the percentages that are listed here might be a little high and that it's OK to lower them until they get their feet on solid financial ground.
Comments/ Extra activities:	Have them redo the SSP using a higher figure, i.e., less taken out for other jars while they are getting started. Let them see that the percentages are only a guide and not hard and fast rules they have to live by. Life is organic and their budgets should be also.
Vocabulary:	Budget, SSP, pay yourself first, gross income, taxes, net income, expenses.

SPENDING AND SAVING PLAN (SSP) (AKA A BUDGET)

Unless you know where you are, it's hard to know how to get where you want to go. A spending and savings plan puts you in charge and gives you a tool with which to reach your dreams. Let's assume you just graduated from college and are making $3000 a month at your first real job or from your first business. Let's fill in the blanks below and get started!

Gross Income
- ❏ From Job - .... $_____

Taxes
- ❏ Federal, State, Social Security, Medicare (32%)........................ $ _____

Net Income (take home pay)
- ❏ GROSS INCOME MINUS TAXES .... $_____

PAY YOURSELF FIRST (MONEY JARS)
- ❏ Living Jar - for needs and wants (55%) - see next page .... $_____
- ❏ Freedom Account (10%)... $_____
- ❏ Saving (10%) .... $_____
- ❏ Education (10%)... $_____
- ❏ Play (10%)... $_____
- ❏ Donations (5%) .... $_____

Expenses

Turn to the next page and fill in the amount you think you might spend on the expenses listed. When you have finished, add up the total and put it in the box below and subtract it from your Living Jar total. If you have money left over, good job! If you didn't have enough, you'll need to go back and look over your expenses to see where you might adjust.

Living Jar total to live on (from above): $1122.00

Subtract your total expenses (from budget on next page): .... $_____

Remainder, if any (put into your Freedom Jar!): .... $_____

Other stuff you might not think of:

- Bank fees
- Bottled water
- Washing your car
- Dentist
- New tires

- Driver's license renewals
- Smog checks
- Laundromats
- Cover charges
- Coffee drinks/smoothies

- Gum
- Office supplies
- Emergencies
- Uniforms
- And on and on and on!!!

It's not as easy as you might think!

TRY YOUR BUDGET SKILLS – REALITY CHECK

Principle/ Lesson:	An SSP or budget is a tool to reach your dreams.
What:	The budget part of the SSP is a way to help plan for expenses. More importantly, it gives you a way to free up some of your money so that you have extra money, also called discretionary income, to invest more for the future if you want.
Why:	Universal Law: If you don't keep track of the money you have or take care of the money that is placed in your care, you won't be given the opportunity to handle any more. It's like a small child who is given a three scoop ice cream cone and drops it on the floor. You wouldn't turn around and give that child another three scoop cone because you know he can't even handle the one scoop yet.
How:	Go over the different categories on the budget page and help your child research prices for local expenses. Use the newspaper, the internet, whatever is handy. Explain Fixed and Variable expenses (fixed being the same amount each month like rent or your cable bill and variable being expenses like food, gas for your car, etc.). Also, have them circle whether the expense is a need or a want. The object is to see if they can figure out how to live on $1122 a month (55% of the $2040 net income on the previous page). It's a real reality check for them. **Note to parents**: We're pretty sure your child won't be able to figure out how to live on $1122 (unless they tell you they are going to live at home!). You can also look at how much money they would have to earn or make to be able to live the lifestyle they designed on the SSP.
Comments/ Extra activities:	Let your child see your budget and explain to them how you manage your finances. If you don't have a current budget (and we recommend modifying a budget when either your income or expenses change), we would highly suggest you spend some time putting one together and having your child or children help you. Make it a regular family activity. When you plan family activities, letting your children be part of the budget process makes it a team project instead of parents having to constantly saying "no" to kids' wants while you're saving up for something or just needing to cut back for one reason or another.
Vocabulary:	Fixed expense, variable expense, lifestyle, insurance, renter's insurance, health insurance, discretionary income.

TRY YOUR BUDGET SKILLS - REALITY CHECK

EXPENSES	Options ($)		F V	AMOUNT ($)	N W
Shelter	Low	High	Fixed/ Variable		Need or Want
Apartment - one bedroom			F V		N W
Apartment - share two bedroom			F V		N W
Rent room in home			F V		N W
Transportation					
Car (new/used), gas, insurance			F V		N W
Bike			F V		N W
Public Transportation			F V		N W
Food					
Groceries (eat at home)			F V		N W
Eating out			F V		N W
Utilities					
Phone/Cell Phone			F V		N W
Electricity			F V		N W
Gas			F V		N W
Cable TV			F V		N W
Internet (cable or DSL)			F V		N W
Garbage/water			F V		N W
Insurance					
Renter's			F V		N W
Health (often provided by employer)			F V		N W
Personal/Lifestyle					
Clothing			F V		N W
Entertainment (movies, games)			F V		N W
Hair cuts, manicures, etc.			F V		N W
Newspapers, books, magazines			F V		N W
Pets (food, vet, grooming)			F V		N W
Personal Hygiene (soap, shampoo)			F V		N W
Lessons (sports, music, other)			F V		N W
Classes (not college)			F V		N W
Cleaning, household supplies			F V		N W
Other			F V		N W
Other			F V		N W
TOTAL					

WHAT IT COSTS TO RAISE YOU

CHILDREN/PETS ARE EXPENSIVE!

Principle/ Lesson:	Awareness is a powerful tool. Financial education is a family affair.
What:	Most kids are shocked and surprised when they find out how much money their parents spend to raise them. Maybe if young adults knew how expensive it was to raise children, they would plan them better.
Why:	This activity is a real eye opener for kids. We have kids take this sheet home during our Camp Millionaire camps and they will fill them out with their parents. The next day the comments are generally that they had no idea it cost that much to raise them. Most kids in our camps come back the next day and say, "I didn't realize how lucky I was." Even kids whose parents don't have a lot of money are shocked at how much money their parents DO spend on them.
How:	Have your child guess how much you spend each year on the various expenses and then give them the 'real' figures. If you don't know the real figures, it's the perfect time to admit it and let your child help you figure it out. The second section asks you to go over the miscellaneous expenditures with your child so they can really see how much money it costs to raise them.
Comments/ Extra activities:	This is a great opportunity to evaluate what you spend on your child(ren) and let them see how frustrating it can be for you when they constantly ask for stuff that you can't afford YET.
Vocabulary:	Cost, spend, yearly expenses.

WHAT IT COSTS TO RAISE YOU!

Do you have any idea what your parents will spend to raise you from birth to age 17? Probably not. Most statistics on the internet estimate a whopping **$233,000** to raise a child from birth to 17! Maybe this will make you think twice before you beg your parents for piddlyjunk!

<u>Your Guess</u>   <u>Reality</u>

Each year my family spends _____ on housing for me.   _____

Each year my family spends _____ on food for me.   _____

Each year my family spends _____ on clothing for me.   _____

Each year my family spends _____ on health care for me.   _____

Each year my family spends _____ on childcare & education. _____

Each year my family spends _____ on our car expenses.   _____

Now, let's look at some of the miscellaneous things your parents buy for you...

1. My newest pair of sneakers or shoes cost _____?

2. It cost _____ to have my teeth cleaned this year.

3. I get _____ for lunch or snack money each week?

4. The last time I went to a movie it cost _____?

5. My last sport/music lesson cost my parents _____?

6. My newest piece of clothing cost _____?

7. What does it cost your parents to take you to the doctor _____?

8. What is your share of the last family vacation _____?

9. What did it cost your parents this year for birthday and Christmas presents _____?

10. How much money are your parents putting away every month for your college education _____?

11. What did it cost last time you got your hair cut _____?

12. What did it cost your parents last time you went to a birthday party_____?

And this is just a drop in the bucket!
This is the reason it's important to create a budget and stick to it!

PAYING FOR STUFF – USING YOUR MONEY	
Principle/ Lesson:	If you can't afford it in cash, you can't afford it at all!
What:	There are two ways to buy things: 1) Using your own money, or, 2) Using other people's money. It's almost always easier for people of all ages to spend someone else's money. The problem with this is that other people need you to pay that money BACK!
Why:	It's important for children to understand WHERE money comes from for purchases you make while they are young. Your children see you pay for things using different methods: cash, checks, debit cards and credit card, but they don't have an understanding of WHOSE money it is that you are spending or where the money is coming from. This explanation gives your child another way to look at the money that's being spent.
How:	Using the list, go over the ways you commonly pay for things as an adult. Talk about when you use each one, the advantage and/or disadvantage of each one. Have a conversation about how paying for things now is different than it was when you were their age (i.e., younger!).
Comments/ Extra activities:	We want children to understand the difference between using their money and other people's money (OPM) to buy things. When we get into the use of credit cards, they will begin to see the dangers of using OPM to pay for things unless they are assets that have the potential of creating a passive income (cash flow) stream for them.
Vocabulary:	Cash, checks, debit cards, automatic payments.

USING YOUR OWN MONEY

There are several ways to pay for stuff:

Cash

Checks

Debit Cards

Cashier's Check from Bank

Money Order

If you can't afford to pay CASH for it,
you can't afford to buy it, Period!

COUNTING CHANGE BACK	
Principle/ Lesson:	Knowledge is power.
What:	Counting change back is a basic skill every child should learn to do without the aid of a calculator.
Why:	Because most of the retail market uses cash registers that tell you how much change you give back to each customer, employees often don't learn how to 'think' through giving change back. This is especially important when dealing with counting change back as illustrated in the activity.

Even if you always buy things at stores where calculators in cash registers tell employees how much change you should be getting from a purchase when you don't have the exact change, it's important that you make sure you get the correct change. |
| **How:** | Using real money, pretend to buy things using the amounts in the activity.

If you have trouble, try watching this simple YouTube video on counting back change: https://www.youtube.com/watch?v=c-Kooo4gXo8 |
| **Comments/ Extra activities:** | Next time you take your child to the store and you use cash to purchase an item, let him or her figure out what the change would be. |
| **Vocabulary:** | Change. |

COUNTING CHANGE BACK

Let's say, for example, that you purchase an a shirt that costs $12.35.

There are several ways you could pay cash for this item:

1. You could give the checkout person the exact change.

2. You could offer a $20 bill and get back _____.

3. You could offer $20.35 and you'd get back _____.

4. You could offer $22.35 and you'd get back _____.

The trick is to count back the change starting with the smallest coins and bills first and then move to the next smallest and so on.

For example, with #2 above, you would hand the customer back a nickle and say "$12.40", then a dime and say, "$12.50", then two quarters and say, "$13.00", then two $1 bills and say "$15.00" and finally a $5 bill and say, "$20.00."

OK, you try it now...

MONEY CIRCULATION – MONEY IS ENERGY

Principle/ Lesson:	Money is energy, that's why we call it currency. Money represents people's time and energy as well as the value they place on something.
What:	This less introduces the ways in which money circulates in the world, beginning with getting a paycheck. Money is simply energy; we exchange our time and energy for money and then exchange our money for things we need and want. For example, it takes a lot of energy to produce an apple (time, sunshine, fertilizer, water, labor, gas to power the tractor, etc.) and when you exchange your time and energy for money and then turn around and buy an apple, you are simply exchanging energy for energy.
Why:	Understanding how money circulates gives your child a way to see his role in the world in terms of how his money circulates and what it buys. Let him see that the time and energy he spends 'earning' money and then buying things with that money is simply an exchange of energy. Teach him to evaluate the importance of what he wants to trade his time and energy for, i.e., how he 'spends' his time. Let him see how much time HE has to spend in order to buy certain things. In other words, if he earns $10/hour at a job and wants to save up to buy a $100 bike, he will have to work more than 10 hours (because of taxes) to earn enough money to buy the bike. Is the bike 'worth' working those 10 hours for?
How:	Starting with getting paid, walk your child through the pictures, explaining each stop along the way.
Comments/ Extra activities:	Talk to your child about your own paycheck; what route it takes, what happens to the money along the way. Is there money deducted for your retirement account (Freedom Jar), do you have automatic payments taken out for a car or house loan, etc.? The book, *Your Money or Your Life* is a great option here. You may need to explain the joke!
Vocabulary:	Circulation, electronic, debit, paycheck.

How Your Money Circulates

Money as Energy (electronic - no money actually changes hands)

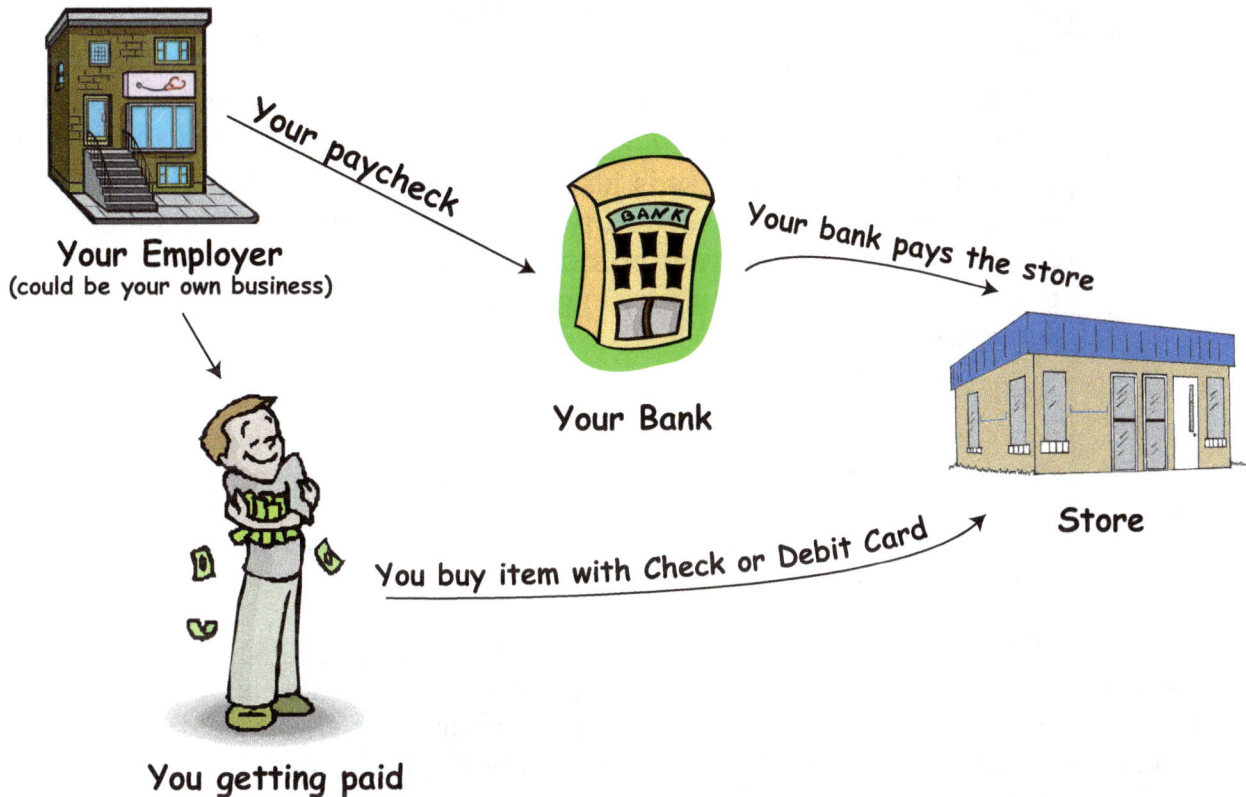

Your Employer
(could be your own business)

Your paycheck

Your Bank

Your bank pays the store

Store

You buy item with Check or Debit Card

You getting paid

JOKE!

An old man was on his death bed. He wanted badly to take all his money with him. He called his priest, his doctor and his lawyer to his bedside. "Here's $30,000 cash to be held by each of you. I trust you to put this in my coffin when I die so I can take all my money with me."

At the funeral, each man put an envelope in the coffin. Riding away in a limousine, the priest suddenly broke into tears and confessed that he had only put $20,000 into the envelope because he needed $10,000 for a new baptistery. "Well, since we're confiding in each other," said the doctor, "I only put $10,000 in the envelope because we needed a new machine at the hospital which cost $20,000."

The lawyer was aghast. "I'm ashamed of both of you," he exclaimed. "I want it known that when I put my envelope in that coffin, it held my personal check for the full $30,000."

WRITING CHECKS	
Principle/ Lesson:	I spend my money wisely. A check is essential a contract between you and the person you bought something from.
What:	Checks are a way to pay for things using your own money that you've put into a checking account at a bank. While it's not paper money, it represents the money you have in the bank in your own name.
Why:	It's important for kids to understand the different ways of paying for things. It's also important that they learn how to write a check and what the check represents even if they will rarely write a check in the future.
How:	Explain that writing checks is just one way you can buy things using your own money. Writing a check is a type of contract called a Promissory Note where you say to the person or store you're writing the check to that you promise there is enough money in your checking account to pay for the purchase. Walk through the steps necessary to write a check, explaining the various parts: name and address, date, pay to line, the amount in numbers, spelling the amount out in words, the memo line and finally the signature. Explain the numbers on the bottom: bank routing number, bank account number, check number. Now have your child write out his own check.
Comments/ Extra activities:	If you still write checks for certain monthly expenses, let your child help you pay these bills, making sure to have him write the amounts in the check register (see the next page in the Playbook), deducting and adding in the amounts of checks written, deposits, fees, etc.
Vocabulary:	Checks, contract, promissory note, check register, deducting, deposits.

When you pay for something with a **CHECK,** you are entering into a **CONTRACT** called a **PROMISSORY NOTE**. This means that you **PROMISE** there is enough money in your checking account to cover the amount of the check.

If you don't have enough money in your account (which is called "insufficient funds" or NSF) your check will **BOUNCE.** Not only will the bank charge you an NSF fee but the person or store you wrote the check to can charge you a **LARGE** fee for bouncing the check.

Sample Check

```
Your Name                                                    1809
Your Address
Your City, State, Zip


                                              January, 1 03
                                     _____

Pay to the order of Person you're writing the check to (Payee)  $  26.89
                                                                   _____

Twenty Six and 89/100 ----------------------------------- Dollars


                                     Sign your Autograph here!
                                     _____
Memo: _____              Signature
  -:323274270-: 0 224732  901  1809
```

You try one!

```
Your Name                                                    1809
Your Address
Your City, State, Zip


                                     _____ , _____


Pay to the order of _____  $ _____
                                                          Dollars
_____


                                     _____
Memo: _____              Signature
  -:323274270-: 0 224732  901  1809
```

WARNING: Never have your social security number, phone number or driver's license number printed on your checks. It's too easy for potential identity thieves to get your information!

YOUR CHECKBOOK REGISTER	
Principle/ Lesson:	I spend my money wisely. I am a excellent money manager.
What:	The checkbook register is the most critical aspect of writing checks because if you don't keep track of where your money is going, it will all be gone before you know it. The challenge in the current digital age, however, is that very few people carry around a check book register.
Why:	Too many people don't keep track of where they spend their money or how much they spend. They write checks or use their debit cards and forget to write the purchase in their check register or a money notebook of some type. The online apps make it way too easy not to keep track of where your money is going. Add to this the fact that so many people don't use a budget and you have a high percentage of the population who spend their entire paychecks and never get around to saving and investing for the future. When you use a debit card, you need to think of that purchase the same as writing a check and make sure to record the transaction in a register or money notebook. With the popular use of automatic deposits and payments, direct deposit paychecks and online bill paying, it is far too easy to forget to put a deposit or payment into the check register. This makes it impossible to keep track of how much money you have and easy to overspend.
How:	Walk your child through recording all the transactions (1-7), adding and subtracting as necessary.
Comments/ Extra activities:	Show your child your own checkbook register (if you have one). Have them help you pay bills and let them write the transactions down, adding and subtracting as necessary. Even if you don't use a register, please find one in order to let your child see how the concept works and have them practice keeping track of their own money to learn the habit. If your child is starting to pay for things himself (which we encourage using the unique allowance system spelled out in The Ultimate Allowance book), we encourage you to start a checking account for your child. Let him have a debit card but supervise the use of it until you know he is being responsible with it and is using a register to keep track of purchases and deposits.
Vocabulary:	Checkbook register, ATM, automatic, description, balance, NSF, writing fee.

YOUR CHECKBOOK REGISTER

ALWAYS use your checkbook register when you write a check or use your DEBIT CARD to keep track of the money you are spending. Write the following transactions in the register below:

1. 2/21   Deposit at ATM - got check for birthday $ 200.00
2. 2/22   Automatic Payment to The Gym for membership $ 50.00
3. 2/29   Payroll deposit into checking account from work $1300.00
4. 3/09   Debit card payment at Alex's Shirt Shop $ 30.00
5. 3/17   Check #1234 - Brown Property Management - Rent $ 700.00
6. 3/27   Debit card payment at Drug Store $ 40.00
7. 3/28   Check #1236 - Gas Company $ 35.00

Date	Check No	Description	✓	Payment	Deposit	Balance
Write beginning balance in here						$1000.00

A NOTE ABOUT BANK FEES:

Many banks offer Free Checking Accounts (no monthly fee) so be sure to shop around. Ask about other fees also, such as NSF (bounced check) fees, wiring fees, etc.

CHECKING ACCOUNT BANK STATEMENT

Principle/ Lesson:	You need to know how much money you have and where your money is going so you can make sure it's doing what it's told. If you don't know where you are, you'll have a difficult time figuring out how to get to where you want to go. You are 100% responsible for financial mistakes, regardless of who makes them...you or your bank.
What:	A checking or savings account bank statement is how you figure out if the amount of money YOU think is in your accounts matches the amount your bank says is in your accounts. Banks and investment companies send out monthly statements so you can keep a close eye on the balances (amount of money) in your accounts. While banks prefer to send you an email letting you know that your monthly statement is ready to download from your account online, by having it sent via mail, you will always have a printed copy to review. Too many people never look at their statements and then they wonder why they get into financial trouble.
Why:	People makes financial mistakes all of the time. Banks make financial mistakes once in a while. If you don't review your statements each month, you can easily miss a mistake and it's challenging at times to go back several months to figure out or remember what happened. Keeping a close eye on your money, i.e., bank accounts, is the only way to make sure it's working as hard as it can for you. If you don't take care of the money you have now, how are you ever going to take care of more?
How:	Walk through the bank statement, comparing it to the previous Playbook activity and then balance it at the bottom following the directions. Though most kids won't ever do this because they will bank online, it's important that they understand the concept. Let them know that financially savvy people still balance their statements every month.
Comments/ Extra activities:	Remember, as a parents, your job is to set the best example possible so have your child help you balance your statements each month on paper so they get the hang of it. And if you aren't in the habit of balancing your accounts, this is a great time to start!
Vocabulary:	Bank statement, balance, reconcile, service fee, automatic payment.

Look at your bank statement EVERY month so that you can stay on top of mistakes that you or the bank make (and banks do make mistakes). Most banks offer access to your accounts online so you can check deposits, withdrawals, interest, etc., whenever you wish.

BANK ACCOUNT STATEMENT FOR:

Frizzy Lizzy

21 Garden Lane

Santa Barbara 93121

Creative Wealth Bank

STATEMENT DATE:

March 31, 2003

Acct. # 000 4564777

ACTIVITY SUMMARY

Beginning Balance...$1000.00
Deposits $1500.00
Withdrawals $911.00
Ending Balance..$1589.00

DEPOSITS

2/21	ATM Deposit Mach ID 0641c Main Branch............	$200.00
2/29	Star Reg Payroll Lizzy, Frizzy......................	$1300.00
	Total deposits	$1500.00

WITHDRAWALS (check/ATM/debit card/automatic payments)

2/22	Automatic Payment - The Gym	$50.00
3/09	Debit Card Purchase - Alex's Shirt Shop.............	$30.00
3/15	Monthly Service Fee	$6.00
3/17	Check # 1234 Brown Property Mgmt - Rent..........	$700.00
3/20	Check # 1235 Ralphs Groceries.....................	$50.00
3/27	Debit card purchase - Drug Store	$40.00
3/28	Check # 1236 Gas Company	$35.00
	Total withdrawals.................................	$911.00

BALANCING / RECONCILING YOUR ACCOUNT

Write the balance in your checkbook register on this line _____

ADD deposits and interest not in register +_____

SUBTRACT checks, debit card purchases, fees not in register -_____

EQUALS Bank Statement Ending Balance (see above) =_____

PAYING FOR STUFF – USING OTHER PEOPLE'S MONEY (OPM)

Principle/ Lesson:	I only borrow money when it's going to make me money. If you can't afford it in cash, you can't afford it at all. Interest is only interesting when you're receiving it.
What:	Using other people's money to buy things is easy but it often costs a lot more in the end. You can't use someone else's money without paying them a fee, called interest, for using it.
Why:	A recent study showed that more than 50% of all Americans spend more than they earn each month. They can only do this by using credit cards and getting loans to buy things. Because buying things on credit is so easy, and because Americans seem to have developed an inability to practice the concept of financial planning and delayed gratification, people find themselves in debt quickly if they aren't careful. Millions find themselves so deep in debt that the only solution is to file for bankruptcy. It's important, also, to know that more college students drop out of college for financial reasons than academic reasons. By teaching kids to avoid credit cards in college (use debit cards instead) and truly evaluate their ability to repay college loans before taking them out, you give them an important advantage after they graduate from college.
How:	Go over the different types of cards, i.e., ways people borrow money, listed on the next page. If you need to know more, please check the glossary in the back of the book. Explain the concept of interest if your child doesn't understand it. Use the analogy of renting a car or home where you have to pay a fee to use them. When you use a credit card, you are literally renting the money from the credit card company. A secured card is used just like a credit card but the person has given the credit card company money to hold in a special account just in case they can't make their payments. Secured cards are often used by people with poor credit to raise their credit rating. Explain credit rating as listed.
Comments/ Extra activities:	Ask your child if they know what a shark is. Explain to them what a loan shark is and why it's so easy for them to make a lot of money on people who are desperate to get money. You can also talk about check cashing stores (for people without bank accounts) and short-term loan businesses. Visit the three credit rating websites for more information and let your child watch you check your own credit rating.
Vocabulary:	OPM, mortgage, charge card, credit card, secured card, loan shark, credit, rental fee, credit rating, bankruptcy.

USING OTHER PEOPLE'S MONEY

Credit Cards

Charge Cards

Secured Cards

Mortgage (real estate loan)

Car Loans

Personal Loans

Credit Line

Q: What is this? $$$

👉 If you can't afford to pay CASH for something when you want to buy it, you can't afford to buy it, Period!

INTEREST (interest is only interesting when you are RECEIVING it!)

Interest is the FEE you have to pay to use other people's money. Think of it like renting a car. You pay the car rental business to 'rent' or use their car for a certain period of time. When you buy something on CREDIT, you pay a RENTAL FEE to the credit card company.

CREDIT RATING - Your financial report card which shows how well you pay for things and manage your money. Your credit rating determines how much money you can borrow and what interest rate you pay. A better credit rating means you can borrow more at a lower interest rate.

NOTE: Just because you can doesn't mean you should!

A: Loan Shark - someone who loans others money and charges VERY high interest rates.

Credit Rating Websites: Experian.com, Equifax.com and TransUnion.com

STEREO SCENARIO

Principle/ Lesson:	If you can't afford it in cash, you can't afford it at all.
	Your financial habits always add up in the end.
	Only use a credit card to pay for things when you know you have the money to pay it in full when you get the bill.
What:	The real cost of borrowing money is often shocking when people add up the interest they paid by the time they pay off their credit card bills.
	It's important to figure in the interest you may have to pay when choosing to purchase piddlyjunk using credit (someone else's money).
	Note: Using credit to purchase something that actually makes you money can be a good thing. More on that later!
Why:	It's so easy to get and use a credit card, but not so easy to fully understand the ramifications or consequences of not paying credit card bills off each month.
	It's important to understand the real cost of using credit cards or other people's money.
How:	Walk through the following scenario and watch the surprise when the kids see how long it would take and how much it would really cost if they only paid the minimum amount due each month to pay off just $1000.
Comments/ Extra activities:	If you have credit card debt, share your situation, how you got into it and how you're getting out it with your child.
	If you are in debt and don't yet have a plan for getting out of debt, please consider taking this crucial step and letting your child be part of the process. It's an incredible learning opportunity for you both. And don't worry...they won't think less of you. Children actually feel better when they realize their parents aren't perfect!
	And remember, children learn best by example so make sure you're setting the best example possible for your children.
Vocabulary:	Credit card, rent, borrow, minimum payment, interest.

THE REAL COST OF USING CREDIT CARDS!

What it costs to BORROW (rent) money from others

Let's say you decide you want a new stereo (or bike or laptop or phone or _____) which costs $1000. You find the one you want and decide to charge the amount on your credit card instead of saving up and paying cash for it. When you get the bill, you have two options:

1. Pay it off completely with money in your savings account, IF you have been saving up for it, or;

2. Make monthly payments until it's paid off.

This is what you'd end up paying for the stereo (original cost of $1000) if you only made the minimum payment of $20 each month (at 18% interest) AND it would take you 19.3 years to pay it off this way!

$2931.00!!! - OUCH

How much extra did you pay for the stereo when you charged it on a credit card and only made the minimum payment?_____

TOO many people do this...will you?

MONEY CIRCULATION – CREDIT CARDS

Principle/ Lesson:	Money is energy.
What:	When you buy something using a credit card (other people's money), it's actually the credit card company that pays the store. When you get your monthly statement from the credit card company, you have the option of paying it off in full or paying it off in payments with interest.
Why:	It's important for kids to understand who is actually buying those jeans or movies when they use a credit card. All kids normally see is their parents USING the credit cards. They don't see the whole picture.
How:	Walk through the diagram on the next page starting with the person getting paid, then buying something with a credit card, then having the credit card company pay the store and finally the person paying the credit card company the amount of the purchase plus interest.
Comments/ Extra activities:	Show your child one of your credit card statements, the minimum payment due, the due date and billing cycle, interest rate, amount of interest, etc. Have them read all of the small print on the back of the card and on the statement and have a discussion about what they read. Have your child do an internet search for credit card comparisons and see what comes up. Compare different types of cards, credit lines, types of billing methods, grace periods, etc. Have a conversation about 'points' and 'miles'. Explain that points and miles are worthless if you can't pay off your bill every month. You simply end up paying more money just to get points. If you know someone who has gotten themselves into, or is currently in, serious credit card debt, ask that person if they'll have lunch (and pay with cash!) with your child to share that experience with them. There is nothing like hearing a personal account to impact a child for life.
Vocabulary:	Circulation, credit card, principal, interest.

How Your Money Circulates
Paying by Credit/Charge Card

Technically, when you use a credit card to buy something, you are 'renting' someone else's money. They will charge you a rental fee (% of purchase) called INTEREST if you don't pay the full amount you charged when you get the credit card bill. The amount you 'borrowed' is called the PRINCIPAL.

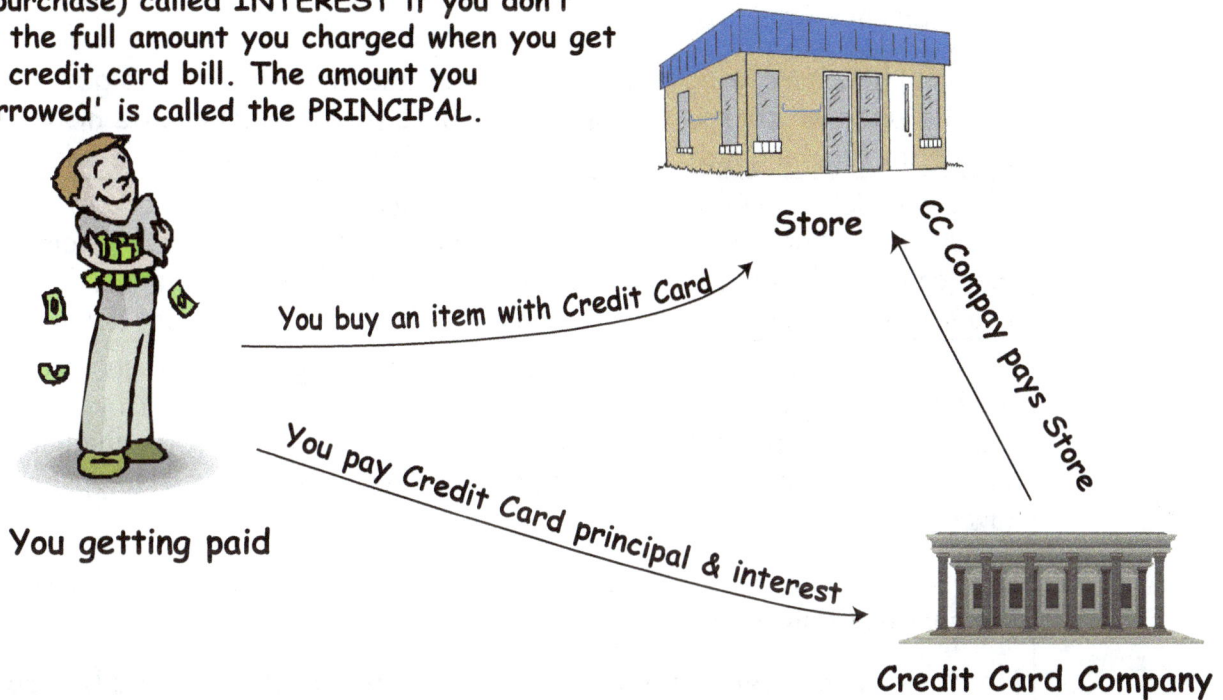

Store

CC Compay pays Store

You buy an item with Credit Card

You getting paid

You pay Credit Card principal & interest

Credit Card Company

JOKE!

After weeks of getting the cold shoulder from his wife, an unhappy husband finally confronted her.

"Admit it, Linda," he said, "The only reason you married me is because my grandfather left me $10 million."

"Don't be ridiculous!" She shot back. "I don't care who left it to you."

CREDIT CARDS 101 - PLASTIC MONEY	
Principle/ Lesson:	Only borrow money when it's going to make you money. If you can't afford it in cash, you can't afford it at all. The first step in taking control of your money is to stop borrowing money. (Dave Ramsey)
What:	Credit and debt go hand and hand and in first world countries, children are raised to think that borrowing money is a normal way of life. That is our first financial wrong thought...that it's a perfectly normal thing to borrow money from others. It's NOT! Learning how borrowing money affects us and how easy it is to get into trouble when we borrow money from others (use other people's money) is critical to teaching kids how to grow into financially responsible adults.
Why:	If young adults don't understand the consequences of using credit cards to buy things they want, instead of using them for REAL emergencies, they can quickly get themselves into debt. And that debt can quickly turn into stress and overwhelm they can't handle financially or emotionally.
How:	Open up the conversation with your child by asking them the questions on the following page. Be prepared to be perfectly honest with your children...this is the only way they learn. If you're in debt, be open about how it affects you and the whole family. If you use credit wisely, share how you learned to do this. Let them ask any question they want about this topic and just see where the conversation takes you. Next, simply go over the next four pages as you feel your child is ready, again, be open to conversation and questions.
Comments/ Extra activities:	If you can get ahold of a credit card application, have your child try to read all of the fine print!
Vocabulary:	Credit, debt, credit cards, interest.

CREDIT CARDS 101 – PLASTIC MONEY

1) What does the word CREDIT mean? _____

_____

2) What does the word DEBT mean? _____

_____

3) What is a CREDIT CARD? _____

_____

4) Where do you get a CREDIT CARD? _____

_____

5) Why do people get CREDIT CARDS? _____

_____

6) If someone handed you $1000 and told you that you were free to spend it any way you wanted, how would that make you feel? _____

_____

7) How would you feel if after you spent it on something, the person told you they needed the $1000 back plus a rental fee, aka INTEREST, for using their money?

_____

_____

8) What if you spent the $1000 but couldn't pay it back and each month you couldn't pay it back, the rental fee for using that person's money increased? Now how do you feel? Would you feel stressed? What could you do if you got into this situation?

_____

_____

This is exactly what a credit card is AND how adults get into financial trouble every day. They use someone else's money to buy things they can't afford to pay for in cash, and then find themselves in a situation where they can't pay the money back quickly.

Did you know that more married couples get divorced because of financial trouble than anything else? Just something to think about.

Credit cards can be convenient, but using them wisely is not that simple. They can actually get you into deep financial trouble if you don't know your way around them, so here are some basics to get you started.

Advantages:

- Credit cards offer protection against theft of your cash.
- You can buy items and services you need when you need them, even if you don't have enough cash for them.
- Credit cards can be lifesavers, and your parents may want you to carry a credit card to pay for gas, repairs, emergency phone calls, etc.
- Managing your credit cards well can build a solid credit history for the future.
- If you can use credit responsibly, you'll end up a smarter money manager.

Disadvantages:

- Credit cards make it too easy to buy things you can't afford and can't easily pay for.
- It's tempting to buy on impulse and forget you're actually spending money you must pay back later, or that you're spending future income that you don't have (and may never have!).
- If you only pay the minimum payment each month, it can take years to pay off the balance, and accumulating interest on that balance can make what you bought cost much more in the long run.
- If you fall behind on your credit card bills, it can damage your credit rating and make it harder for you to get loans in the future.

Types Of Credit Cards

Most credit cards provide "unsecured" credit. This means they are lending you money based on your promise to pay back the debt. Credit cards come in several varieties:

- **Charge Cards,** such as American Express or Diner's Club. These are primarily used by businesses and consumers for business expenses and have an large annual fee. Most must be paid off in full each month. Often no spending limit.

- **Bank Cards,** such as Master Card, Visa, and Discover. These credit cards are given by individual banks and can be used to pay for any types of goods and services. Each bank decides credit limits, annual fees, terms and conditions.

- **Company or Retail Store** cards, for department stores and gas stations, can only be used at the retailer who issues them. They have no annual fee, but may have a higher interest rate than bank cards.

Credit History

The way you handle your credit cards affects your credit history. A negative credit history is a serious liability. Credit bureaus keep track of your history and assign you a "credit rating," which can be easily accessed by employers, insurance companies, apartment managers, etc. If you have a poor credit rating, this can keep you from getting things you want, like an apartment or an insurance policy.

As you receive, sign, and use a credit card for the first time, your responsibilities start. Take time to read through the Terms and Conditions that come with a credit card account, and become familiar with what's expected of you.

Here's how to decode the terms:

Annual Fee: This is basically a membership fee for having this credit card account. It will range from $0 (no annual fee) to upwards of $50 or more.

Annual Percentage Rate (APR): The interest rate, expressed per year, applied to your purchases.

Finance Charge: The total amount that you pay to use your credit, which includes interest and any other charges related to the transaction. The credit card company will use one of three methods for calculating the finance charge:

Average Daily Balance Method: Most commonly used. You're credited for a payment from the day the credit company receives it, and then they figure the interest based on the average amount you owed during the previous month.

Adjusted Balance Method: This method benefits you the most and results in the lowest finance charges. The balance is calculated by subtracting the payments and any credits from the balance you owe at the end of the previous billing period.

Previous Balance Method: This method costs you the most. The finance charge is calculated on the balance owed at the end of the previous billing cycle. Payments, credits and new purchases made in the current billing cycle are not included.

Grace Period: The number of days you have before a credit card starts charging you interest on your new purchases. Most credit cards have a 25-55 day grace period. If you pay the full balance before the grace period, you won't be paying any interest on it.

Transaction Fees: Any charge other than a purchase usually carries an extra fee, such as a cash advance, late payment, or going over your credit limit. Some credit cards even charge a monthly fee if you haven't used your card at all.

To stop receiving credit card offers in the mail, call 888-567-8688.

Your Responsibilities:

Every time you purchase something with a credit card, you're entering into a legal agreement with the credit card company, and this is a serious responsibility. Here are some other responsibilities to keep in mind:

- Always keep your cards with you or in a safe place
- Never give your credit card number to friends
- Before signing a receipt, check to see that it's accurate. Destroy all carbon copies. Keep all receipts to check against the billing statement
- Notify the credit card company immediately if you lose your credit card
- Get familiar with the consumer credit laws that protect you

Our Recommendation: If you manage your money properly, you may never need a credit card. Use your debit/ATM card for all your purchases. If you think you want to charge something, remember the test: If you can't afford to pay cash for it, you can't afford it at all! Wait until you've saved up for whatever it is you want and pay cash for it.

However, getting a credit card (especially one that gives you points for travel) when you have a job, using it wisely and paying it off each month will help you develop a positive credit score, but only do this when you are ready and able to handle the responsibility.

YOUR CREDIT SCORE

FICO Scores are the credit scores most lenders use to determine your credit risk.

You have three FICO scores, one for each of the three credit bureaus - Experian, TransUnion, and Equifax and they are usually all a little different, sometimes by as much as 100 points.

Each FICO score is based on the information that each credit bureau keeps on file about you (and the info is often different at each one because they don't share their data with each other).

As the information in each of your credit reports changes, your credit scores tend to change as well.

When you check your FICO scores and credit reports, you are getting a snapshot that is accurate at the time. Remember that as the information in your credit report changes, your FICO scores can also change. We recommend checking all three of your FICO scores and credit reports at least once a year. You're entitled to a free report each year from each of the bureaus but they only give you what's on your report, not your credit rating.

A PERFECT SCORE = 850

The higher your score, the easier it is to:

• Borrow money (loans, credit cards)

• Have lower interest rates

Each credit report lists your:

• Credit accounts (including all credit cards, auto loans, student loans)

• Mortgages (home loans) in your name, including: Creditor and account number, Balance, Date opened, Payment history, Current status, such as "OK," "Closed by customer," "30 days late payment," etc.

• Inquiries: recent applications for new credit

• Collections: when a collection agency is seeking you to repay a debt

• Public Records: court judgments such as a bankruptcy, foreclosure, or tax lien

TIP: Sign up for a free account at www.CreditKarma.com. They will send you notifications each time your credit score changes. For information on your current credit scores, call the following three credit agencies: Equifax 800-525-6285, Experian 888-397-3742 and TransUnion: 800-680-7289.

WHAT IF I MESS UP MY CREDIT SCORE

Everyone makes financial mistakes now and again. It's OK...no one's perfect, nor are you going to get thrown off the planet if you mess up once in a while. They key is to be aware of when you use your credit cards, how you pay your bills, when bills are due, etc.

The BEST way not to mess up with your money is to have a system for spending, savings, paying bills online, etc.

Here is a list of financial things we do that can have an affect on your credit score and your ability to borrow money or use credit in the future. Put a + by the actions that can improve your score and a – by the ones that may decrease your score.

____ Pay your bills on time for many months.

____ Miss a payment.

____ Pay down your debt balances right away or every month.

____ "Max out" your credit cards.

____ Get a new mortgage.

____ Get a new auto loan.

____ Get a new credit card.

____ Get instant credit at a department store.

____ Apply for a new credit card and transfer balances to it.

____ Declare bankruptcy.

____ Use as little credit as possible (unless it's going to make you money!).

____ Pay your credit card off each month (remember, credit card companies use compound interest AGAINST you).

____ Keep the total of your credit limits on all debt sources (cards, mortgages, car loans, personal loans, etc.) much higher than the total amount that you owe.

____ Save up for the things you want.

GOOD DEBT VS. BAD DEBT	
Principle/ Lesson:	Good debt buys assets. Bad debt buys piddlyjunk. Only borrow money when it's going to make you money.
What:	Debt isn't always bad. If debt MAKES you money, it can be a good thing. The way you determine if a debt is good or bad is to ask yourself two questions: 1) Will it make me money, and, 2) Who is making the payments. If it's going to make you money (rent from real estate you purchase or ongoing profit from a business you start) and someone else is making the payments (renter in your rental property or business customers who create a profit for you), then borrowing money is often considered good debt. Good debt usually buys assets that go up in value and bad debt usually buys piddlyjunk that goes down in value.
Why:	Because there's a difference between good debt and bad debt, it's important to be able to tell which is which. One buys assets and usually makes you money; the other buys piddlyjunk and usually costs you money.
How:	Explain the above using the verbiage on this page. Talk to your child about the different debts you may have now and whether or not they are considered good debt or bad debt. If you have some 'bad' debt, explain to your child what your strategy is for getting out of debt.
Comments/ Extra activities:	Have your child try to come up with additional debts and label them good or bad based on the above definition. We've included our Good Debt/Bad Debt Lesson in this program so be sure to check that out. NOTE: Though banks and other financial institutions generally consider a house (or anything owned) an asset, we share Robert Kiyosaki's (from the book *Rich Dad, Poor Dad*) philosophy that a family home (where the family lives) is a liability to the family, not an asset. It's actually the bank's asset. The test is whether or not it would feed you or eat you if you lost your job or source of income. It IS, however, most people's largest investment.
Vocabulary:	Debt, expensive, payments, loaned, indebted.

GOOD DEBT & BAD DEBT

DEBT is an obligation or liability to pay something (in this case money) to someone else.

If you borrow $10 from someone, you have a $10 debt. That person has LOANED you money. You are then INDEBTED to that person.

But what do you do when you want or need to buy something very expensive?

1) Save up for it

2) Get a loan from a bank or other financial institution

3) Use a credit card

The rule of thumb is to borrow money to buy something that is going to MAKE you money (which we call investing in or buying an asset). Never borrow money to buy something that is going to decrease in value.

GOOD DEBT vs. BAD DEBT – Good debt buys assets; Bad debt buys liabilities! Another way to tell if debt is good or bad is to look at who is making the payments. With good debt, someone else is usually making the payments; with bad debt, you are!

Good
Debt

Real Estate

Businesses

Bad
Debt

Automobiles

Coffee drinks

You name some:

_____

_____

_____

You name some:

_____

_____

_____

MONEY CIRCULATION – BUYING BIG TICKET ITEMS

Principle/ Lesson:	Assets feed you, liabilities eat you. Only borrow money when it's going to make you money.
What:	Money you borrow for a major purchase comes from a bank or other lending institution (which is a business that lends money) that pays for the car or the house. You then pay the bank or lending institution monthly payments that include interest on the loan until the loan is paid off in full. Most loans for automobiles, real estate or business have a predetermined number of payments, in other words, you might get a five-year loan to buy a car or a 30-year loan to buy a house.
Why:	It's important to understand where the money comes from when you make a major purchase such as a car or house and also how amortization works.
How:	Explain the word Amortization - the repayment of a loan over time, normally with compound interest (we'll cover this in a bit). In the case of a house or car, that time can be anywhere from 3 years to 5 years (auto loan) or 15 to 30 or more years (house loan or mortgage). Banks are starting to offer even longer time frames because large items are becoming more and more expensive. So, to keep the monthly payments affordable, they spread the payments over a longer period of time. Remember, however, that the longer it takes you to pay off a loan, the more interest you end up paying on that loan.
Comments/ Extra activities:	If you have a car or house loan, show your child a few statements so he can see how the principal decreases over time. Search the internet for an amortization table or calculator to illustrate how a large amortized loan is paid back over time.
Vocabulary:	Circulation, principal, interest, loan, amortization, repayment.

How Your Money Circulates
Getting a Loan for a Major Purchase

When you take out a loan to buy a house or car (or boat or...) you are 'renting' someone else's money for a specified period of time, for example, 5 years (car) or house (15 to 30 years).

You have a set payment every month and if you don't make your payments, the loan company will repossess (take from you) the item you bought. Your monthly payment will include INTEREST (APR or annual percentage rate) and PRINCIPAL (original amount of money you borrowed).

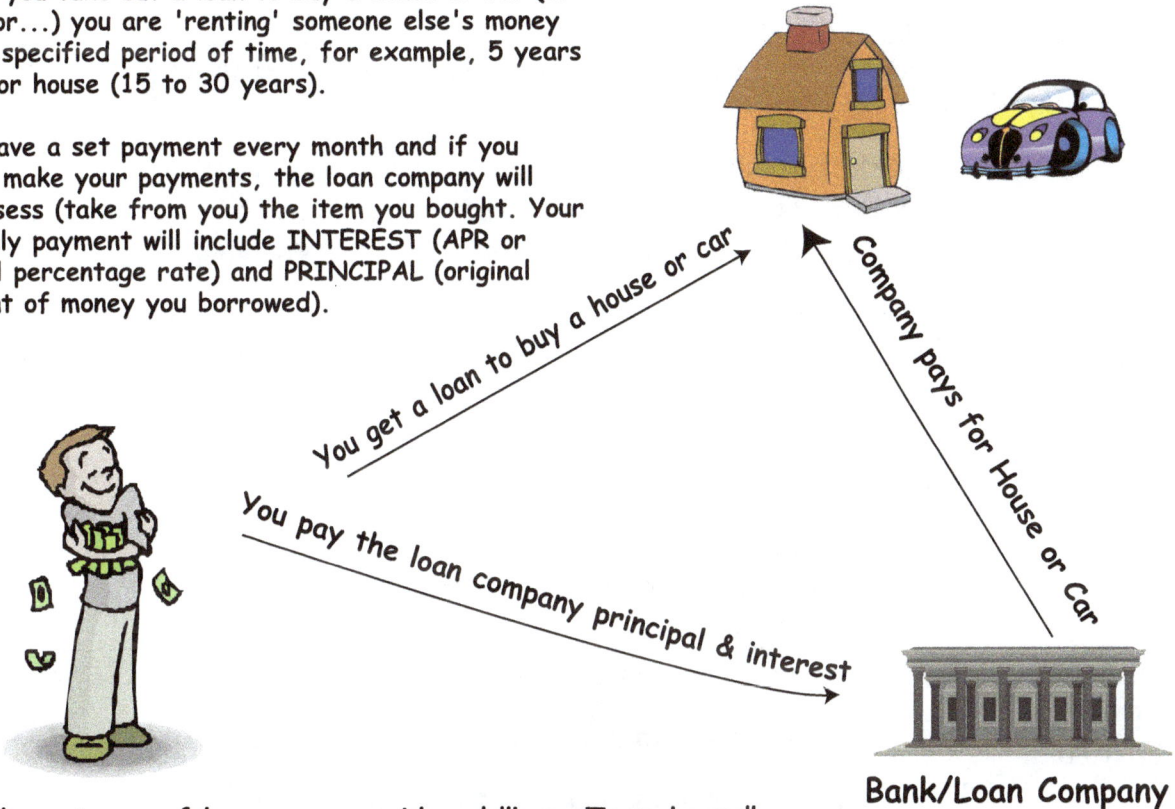

You get a loan to buy a house or car

You pay the loan company principal & interest

Company pays for House or Car

Bank/Loan Company

These types of loans are considered "Long Term Loans"

JOKE!

Reaching the end of a job interview, the Human Resources person asked the hot-shot young Engineer, fresh out of MIT, "And what starting salary were you looking for?" The engineer cooly said, "In the neighborhood of $125,000 a year, depending on the benefits package."

The interviewer said, "Well, what would you say to a package with 5 weeks vacation, 14 paid holidays, full medical and dental, company matching retirement fund to 50% of salary, and a company car leased every 2 years - for starters, say, a red Corvette?"

The engineer tried to control his excitement, but sat straight up and said, "Wow! Are you kidding?"

"Yeah," the interviewer shrugged, "But you started it."

AMORTIZATION – PAYING FOR BIG THINGS OVER TIME

Principle/ Lesson:	Only borrow money when it makes you money.
What:	Amortization is the method of calculating interest on large purchases that are paid back over an extended period of time.
Why:	It's important to understand how interest is figured on a loan so you understand how much of your payment is being applied to principal and how much is being applied to interest.
How:	Show your child how much it costs to use Other People's Money to buy things. Although it is usually unreasonable, but not impossible, to save up enough money to buy a house, it is quite reasonable to put money away each month to save up for a car, especially a used one in great shape. Getting a loan to buy a house is an acceptable way to finance a house but again, it's important to understand how the monthly payment is structured. The amount of interest is based on the amount you owe, also called the principal. As you pay off the loan by making monthly payments, the amount of interest in each payment decreases because you owe less principal. This is called amortization.
Comments/ Extra activities:	If you have a loan that is amortized, show your statements to your child. Also, if your child wants a new car, do this exercise with him: Give him a small piece of paper and tell him to write $7000 on it and spend a good five to ten minutes decorating it (crayons, stickers, etc.). When he is finished, tell him to rip it up and ignore his protests. This is to illustrate that as soon as you drive a new car off the car lot, it depreciates (goes down) in value an average of $7000 because now it is used. The time he spent decorating the piece of paper represents the time it would have taken him to earn the $7000 that he lost.
Vocabulary:	Amortization, principal, interest, depreciation, annual, interest, borrowed, value.

AMORTIZATION – PAYING FOR BIG THINGS OVER TIME

AMORTIZATION means paying back a loan over time with regular payments, usually monthly. These payments are made up of the **PRINCIPAL** (the amount you borrowed) and the **INTEREST** (the rental fee for borrowing the money).

In the beginning of the loan period, your payments are mostly interest because you owe most of the principal. At the end of the loan, your payments are mostly principal because as the amount you owe decreases, so does the interest that is due each month because the interest is calculated on the principal balance of the loan.

Estimates say that the value of a new car drops up to 40% during the first two years you own it!

Let's Buy a New Car!!!

Amount (principal): $35,000

Total Payments: 60

Average interest rate: 6.00%

Monthly Payment: $644.58

REAL COST OF CAR: $38,675

Total Interest Paid = $3,675

Now, let's Buy a House!!!

Amount borrowed (principal): $400,000

Total Payments: 360 (30 years)

Annual interest rate: 4.00%

Monthly payment: $2398.20

REAL COST OF HOUSE:

$863,353 - OUCH!!!

Total Interest Paid = $463,353

This is why BANKS LOVE TO LOAN YOU MONEY to buy REAL ESTATE!

THE LET'S BUY A HOUSE PLAY!

DIRECTIONS:

Gather as many kids as you can to play the following eight roles or have a couple of kids play multiple roles.

CAST OF CHARACTERS
The Commentator
The Buyer
Buyer's Real Estate Agent
The Seller
Seller's real estate Agent
The Banker
Escrow Officer
The Renter

SCENE 1

The Buyer: I want to buy a house. I'm going to make a list of things I want, and then call my realtor.

C: Buyer calls his/her Realtor:

Buyer's Real Estate Agent (on phone): Best Homes Realty, this is Buyer's Real Estate Agent, how can I help you?

The Buyer: I'm in the market for a house.

Buyer's Real Estate Agent: What kind of house are you looking for?

The Buyer: I want a house with 3 bedrooms and 2 baths. I want to be near schools and I want it to be in decent shape. I can afford approximately $250,000.

Buyer's Real Estate Agent: I'll do some research and call you tomorrow with a list of homes we can go see.

SCENE 2 – Three days later at Buyer's Real Estate Agent' office.

Buyer's Real Estate Agent: So, I found three houses I thought might interest you.

The Buyer: How did you find these places?

Buyer's Real Estate Agent: Well, I looked at the MLS listings on my computer. It showed me all the houses in your price range, and I picked out these three. Would you like to see the first one?

The Buyer: Yes, I'm ready now.

C: The Buyer and Buyer's Real Estate Agent drive to HOME A.

Buyer's Real Estate Agent: This house has everything you want. It has three bedrooms and two baths, it's in a good location, close to schools. It doesn't have a garage, but it's got a big backyard. It does need a little fixing up though. The price is $250,000.

The Buyer: It's nice, but I'd still like to see the other two houses you chose.

Buyer's Real Estate Agent: Let's go.

C: They drive to HOME B.

Buyer's Real Estate Agent: This home also has three bedrooms and two baths, plus there is a double car garage. The backyard is pretty small. It's near schools, but far from where you work. The price is $350,000.

The Buyer: Al right, let's see the last one.

C: They drive to HOME C.

C: Now this place is a condo. It has three bedrooms, two baths, and a single car garage. It's in a great location, it's in great shape, and…it has a pool! Price is $300,000.

The Buyer: Thank you Ms. Jones. I really like the condo, but I also see great potential in HOME A. It's in a good location, and if I fix it up I can probably sell it for a profit later. I'll call you when I decide.

SCENE 3

C: The Buyer calls Buyer's Real Estate Agent.

The Buyer (on phone): Buyer's Real Estate Agent, I'd like to make an offer to buy HOME A for $225,000.

Buyer's Real Estate Agent: Al right. Why don't you come into my office. I'll write us an offer for $225,000 to be presented to the sellers. You'll need to put down $5,000 "earnest money." That's to let the sellers know that the offer is a serious one and we aren't just wasting their time. Can you come in tomorrow?

The Buyer: I'll be there.

C: The next day, after The Buyer and Buyer's Real Estate Agent put together the offer, Buyer's Real Estate Agent delivers the offer to the Seller's Real Estate Agent.

Seller's Real Estate Agent (on phone to Seller): Hi, Mr./Ms. Seller. I just received an offer for $225,000 for your home. What do you think?

Mr./Ms. Seller: Hmmm. That a little bit low. Tell them we will counter the offer at $240,000.

Seller's Real Estate Agent: I'll let them know. (Hangs up)

C: Seller's Real Estate Agent looks up Buyer's Real Estate Agent number.

Seller's Real Estate Agent (on phone): Mr./Ms. Seller wants to do a counter offer for $240,000.

Buyer's Real Estate Agent: I'll let The Buyer know.

Mr./Ms. Jones (calls The Buyer on phone): The seller has counter offered $240,000.

The Buyer: That would be fine. Let's do it!

SCENE 4

Buyer's Real Estate Agent: Now that you and the Seller have agreed on the selling price of $240,000, you need to go to the bank and apply for a home loan. You will need to bring with you proof of income, your previous year's tax return, and your personal financial statement.

C: The next day, The Buyer goes to the bank.

The Buyer: Mr. Banker, I need a loan to buy a house.

The Banker: Great. What is the price of the house, and how much of a down payment will you be making?

The Buyer: I plan to put 20% of the purchase price down, or $48,000.

The Banker: Very well. You'll need to apply for a loan of $187,000 plus costs. To process your loan I will need your last two year's tax returns, and a check stub from your employer and you'll need to fill out this home loan application.

C: The Buyer goes home, completes the loan application package, and takes it back to The Banker the next day.

Buyer's Real Estate Agent (on phone to The Buyer): I'll begin to set up Escrow at the Escrow Company. By the way, I also called a home inspector that I trust, and he's done a thorough, four-hour inspection of the home. You'll need to pay him $400 for the inspection, and he has also turned up several things that need to be repaired.

The Buyer: That sounds fine. I'll pay for the repairs myself. Thank you.

C: The next day.

The Banker (on phone to The Buyer): "Congratulations! Your loan has been approved at a 5% interest rate for 30 years."

C: A week later.

Buyer's Real Estate Agent (on phone to The Buyer): The Title Company has issued a preliminary Title Report, which is a report that shows who actually owns the property and house, on the property. Everything is in order. We're going to close Escrow in 30 days.

The Buyer: I'm ready. See you in 30 days.

SCENE 5 - 30 days later

Buyer's Real Estate Agent on phone to Buyer: I just called to let you know that it's been thirty days since we made the offer on your house, and it's time to go to the Escrow company to sign the papers.

The Buyer: Great. I'm so excited!

The Buyer and Buyer's Real Estate Agent go to the Escrow Company, where they meet in a conference room with an Escrow officer.

The Escrow Officer: Here are all the papers you need to sign. I know that it's a lot, but they are all necessary.

C: After an hour or two The Buyer has read and reviewed ever page and has signed all the contracts.

The Buyer: I'm all done signing. The bank has already issued you a check for $188,000, and I have brought my check for $51,000 which will cover the down payment of $48,000 plus the additional closing costs.

The Escrow Officer: Thanks, you're all set.

Buyer's Real Estate Agent: Here are your keys. Enjoy your new home!

C: Seller's Real Estate Agent and Buyer's Real Estate Agent have now both made a commission on the sale.

SCENE 6 - 3 months later

The Buyer: I've lived in this house for a couple of months now, and fixed it up quite nicely. But since my house payments are $1265 a month which includes taxes and insurance, and since I have an extra room, I was thinking I could rent it out and bring in some money to help with the payments.

C: The Buyer puts an ad in the paper for a room for rent for $700.

The Renter (at The Buyer's house): Hi, I saw your ad for a room. I thought I'd like to rent it. Can I take a look at it?

The Buyer: Sure, come on in.

Mr./Ms Renter: This looks great! I'll take it.

The Buyer (to himself/herself): Now that I'm renting out this room for $700, I can put this extra money toward the loan on my house and pay it off quicker. I'm on my way to financial freedom!

The End!

Extra Credit Question: How else could the story have ended? What else can the buyer do with the house?

	BEING A SMART SHOPPER
Principle/ Lesson:	Prior Proper Planning leads to better buying decisions.
What:	Spending money on piddlyjunk (stuff that goes down in value or has no value at all after you buy it), wastes an enormous amount of your financial resources that could be invested (put to work to produce cash flow or appreciation of an asset in value) to attain financial freedom. Learning to be a wise consumer or smart shopper will help your child evaluate his purchasing decisions and waste less of his financial resources.
Why:	Roughly 75% of Americans are said to live month to month, having no money left over at the end of each pay period. The concept of delayed gratification is long gone with the advent and prevalence of credit card use. It's too easy just to 'charge it' now and pay for it later. We've become a society that thinks of the costs of things in terms of $X per month instead of the total cost over time if charged. Since we are so concerned with having all the latest and greatest toys, gadgets, clothes, cars, big houses, etc., it is becoming more and more important to teach kids to save and invest and, when they do spend their hard earned money, to carefully evaluate each purchase. A recent study showed that by the first grade, students recognized over 200 corporate logos so it's easy to understand that they're being raised to be great consumers but not many of them are being taught to be great savers and great investors.
How:	Walk through the questions and steps on this page using a recent want or purchase.
Comments/ Extra activities:	Do this with your child the next time you are in the process of purchasing an item. Let him help you answer the questions.
Vocabulary:	Hourly rate, status cost, warranty, delayed gratification.

BEING A SMART SHOPPER

Questions to ask yourself BEFORE you buy something:

1. How is this 'thing' going to make me feel?

2. Do I NEED it or just WANT it?

3. Can I buy something that would make me money instead?

4. Will this thing INCREASE in value or DECREASE in value?

Name something you bought recently: _____

What did it cost you? _____

How many hours of your life did it cost you? _____ Cost divided by hourly rate.

Example: $200 divided by $10/hour = 20 hours you worked for it! Worth it?

Things to remember when you want to buy something:

- The price of something doesn't always reflect its value or quality.

- A large percentage of every sales price pays for its marketing/advertising. Good examples include athletic shoes, cars and bottled water.

- It's time we started thinking deeper about the purchases we make in terms of their impact on the environment. As yourself what impact you are making to the earth and humanity when you buy something.

Things to think about when shopping for something:

1. Price? (Nothing is free!)

2. Quality?

3. Warranty? What happens if it breaks?

4. Return policy if you change your mind? What if you bought it from a catalog or online?

5. Will it go on sale soon?

6. Will it be out of date soon?

7. Is this an emotional decision? WHY do you want it?

8. What is the STATUS COST of the item?

9. Can I buy it used?

MAKING GOOD BUYING DECISIONS

Principle/ Lesson:	Prior Proper Planning leads to better buying decisions. THINGS rarely make us happy. Choosing happiness every day is what keeps us happy.
What:	This is a system of evaluating whether or not to make a purchase.
Why:	Too often we buy things impulsively instead of taking time to research the product, prices, warranties, etc. This is a great way to evaluate purchases to determine if you've found the best price, best item, etc.
How:	Have your child list something he wanted or needed to buy recently or is thinking of buying soon. Help him compare the price of this item at different stores or on the internet. Help him compare the cost of this item with similar items. Then, using unit pricing (per size, per pound, etc.), help him compare the cost with different sizes of the same product if applicable. Now have him list the positive and negative aspects associated with the purchase. Ask him if the item needs to be new or could a used one work fine. Now list the item being purchased (if still deciding to buy it after evaluating the purchase) and at what price. Finally, ask him if he thinks he made the best decision he could have with the information he had at the time.
Comments/ Extra activities:	Next time your child wants something, have him walk through this process to see if it helps him make a great financial decision.
Vocabulary:	Buying, evaluation, unit pricing.

DECISION TO BUY

List something you want or need to buy _____

DO YOUR COMPARISON SHOPPING (MARKET RESEARCH)

How could you satisfy this need/want & get the most for your money?

1. Compare price for the same item at different stores/online

2. Compare the cost of similar items

3. Use UNIT PRICING (per size, per number), to compare cost of different sizes of the same product.

EVALUATE YOUR ALTERNATIVES

Weigh pluses and minuses of the alternatives:

+_____/_____ -

+_____/_____ -

+_____/_____ -

+_____/_____ -

Ask yourself, "Do I need to buy this item new or would a used one do just fine?" (answer) _____

DECISION TO BUY

You decide which item to buy, where to buy it, how to buy it.

Decision _____ Price _____

POST PURCHASE EVALUATION

Did you make the best decision at the time?

Yes?_____No? _____

"Many a man thinks he is buying pleasure, when he is really selling himself a slave to it." - Benjamin Franklin

ADVERTISING TACTICS COMPANIES USE TO GET YOU TO BUY

Principle/ Lesson:	Advertisers use different emotional tactics to motivate you to buy things you do not need. Money buys stuff, not happiness.
What:	When we think we want to buy something, it is often not the 'thing' that we want but how that thing is going to make us feel, i.e., cooler, smarter, sexier, more popular, taller, etc. It's important to understand this so you know when you're being manipulated into buying something and ALL advertising is manipulative!
Why:	In order to be able to evaluate whether we're making a smart purchase, we need to understand 'why' we want to purchase something. If we can pinpoint the 'why', we can often find another choices (going for a walk, talking to a friend, etc.) that will bring us the same feeling without spending our precious financial resources on something that may only bring us pleasure for a short period of time.
How:	Have your child go through this list of emotions to see if he can name ads he's seen on TV, billboards, clothing, heard on the radio, read in newspaper or magazines, etc., that advertised something using that emotion. This is a fun activity to do with a group of kids (or adults!).
Comments/ Extra activities:	Watch TV, listen to the radio or read magazines or the newspaper and talk about how ads try to get you to feel so you'll spend money.
Vocabulary:	Advertising, tactics.

ADVERTISING TACTICS

Name something you've seen advertised that uses this emotion in an ad.

Use of fear	Lack of something	Security
Popularity	Power	Value
Being new	Freedom	Fun
Humor	Sexy	Convenience
Jingles - music	Comfort	Excitement
Repetition	Health and well-being	Feeling good

MONEY MAKES THE WORLD GO ROUND – SUPPLY AND DEMAND

Principle/ Lesson:	Supply and demand makes the money go around. The value of everything is subjective and based on much people think a certain thing is 'worth'.
What:	Economics is the social science that deals with the production, distribution, and consumption of goods and services and with the theory and management of money or money systems. Supply and demand is the concept that says when the supply of something is greater than the demand for that thing, the price of that thing generally goes down and when supply is less than the demand, the price generally goes up.
Why:	Understanding how the supply of 'stuff,' cost of oil and other natural resources, jobs, etc., affect each other gives your child a way to think through how his decisions, especially purchasing decisions are affected by supply and demand.
How:	Simply go through the page with your child.
Comments/ Extra activities:	Use something your child likes to collect or sell or trade to illustrate supply and demand. Go to the internet and further research supply and demand. Look at the paper if you take it, or stores online on a daily basis to find examples of how the costs of things are affected by the costs of other things: oil, real estate, energy, gas, production of 'stuff' that depends on oil, etc. This can be a complicated topic, even for adults. Just explore the ideas to get an idea about demand, prices, supply, world events, etc.
Vocabulary:	Economics, supply, demand, production, distribution, consumption.

SUPPLY AND DEMAND

The study of **ECONOMICS** deals with how things are made, sold and used by society. Economics is very interesting because it shows how buying, selling, manufacturing, interest rates, etc., are all interrelated and affect each other.

Supply and Demand: the major reason the price (cost) of things goes up or down.

When there is more supply (stuff you can buy) than there is demand (people who want to buy that stuff) the price of things goes...

_____

When there is more demand (people who want to buy stuff) than there is supply (stuff to buy) the price of things goes... _____

"My dad is worried about the economy because Alpo is up to 99 cents a can. That's almost $7.00 in dog money." - Joe Weinstein

THE REAL COST OF THINGS	
Principle/ Lesson:	Things aren't always what they seem. You can't believe everything you see or read. Myth: You get what you pay for. Is this necessarily true?
What:	The fact that one brand of an item costs more than another brand does NOT mean it's better quality.
Why:	In order to help your child decide whether or not to buy something or which thing to buy, it's important to understand all the steps a product goes through before it reaches his hands and everything that makes up the price, i.e.,
How:	Walk your child through this list so he can see everything that goes into the final cost of a pair of running shoes when it gets to the customer in a retail store. NOTE: This example was taken from the internet and is based on 1995 numbers but the same steps happen today.
Comments/ Extra activities:	Have your child search the internet for other examples of this concept. If you have a friend or relative who makes and distributes a product, let your child talk to them about what it costs to bring the product to market.
Vocabulary:	Cost, consultants, executives, customs, operating profit, promotion, research.

THE REAL COST OF THINGS!

See the costs in 1995 of a pair of $70 Brand Name Shoes "Air Pegasus" shoes. The data was compiled by researchers at the Washington Post newspaper using information from Brand Name Shoes, the US Customs Service, a large national retail chain, the Athletic Footwear Association, industry consultants and executives. All costs are in US dollars. (Washington Post, 1995)

Production labor	$2.75
Materials	$9.00
Rent, equipment	$3.00
Supplier's operating profit	$1.75
Duties	$3.00
Shipping	$.50
Cost to Brand Name Shoes	$20.00
Research and development	$.25
Promotion and advertising	$4.00
Sale's distribution, administration	$5.00
Brand Name Shoes's operating profit	$6.25
Cost to retailer	$35.00
Retailer's rent	$9.00
Personnel	$9.50
Other	$7.00
Retailer's operating profit	$9.00
COST TO CONSUMER	$70.00

"Advertising may be described as the science of arresting the human intelligence long enough to get money from it."
– Unknown

ETHICS - RIGHT VS. WRONG, OR RIGHT VS. RIGHT?

Principle/ Lesson:	Most people know how to judge between right vs. wrong. The challenge, and hard decisions, are choosing between two rights.
What:	The topic of ethics is an important one to introduce to kids at any age. It is as important in interpersonal relationships as it is in business relationships. It's often more difficult to make a choice between right and *right* than it is between right and wrong. We inherently know right from wrong, but choosing between right vs. right, as in the example given, is often a lot more challenging.
Why:	Giving children tools with which to make ethical decisions in life is invaluable. Since all of life involves relationships with others, learning to tell the truth and be authentic to oneself is important to a person's growth and maturity and finding one's place in the world.
How:	Introduce the concept of ethics. Have your child look it up in the dictionary or on the internet. Have him read the dilemma in the box and let him tell you how he would decide if and when he would tell an adult.
Comments/ Extra activities:	Talk about different decisions you've had to make in the recent past or at any point in your life that was both between right vs. wrong and right vs. right. Ask him if he can think of any situation where he'd had to or have to choose between two right values. Have him circle the five values on the page that are most important to him. Do this with your child and talk about your own values as well. NOTE: The five universal values that show up in almost every culture are: honesty, respect, responsibility, compassion, fairness.
Vocabulary:	Ethics, dilemma, values, all the value words, authentic.

ETHICS 101

ETHICS is the set of principles of right conduct. What does that mean? It means making the right best decision (there may be more than one) when you are faced with a dilemma (when you don't know what to do).

Your Dilemma:

What if your best friend swore you to secrecy but was about to do something that might harm him/her, or someone else, seriously? How do you decide if, and when, you should tell an adult?

DO YOU KNOW THE DIFFERENCE BETWEEN

RIGHT vs. WRONG?
RIGHT vs. RIGHT?

Ethical decisions are usually made in line with the things you think are valuable or important. Circle the VALUES that mean the most to you.

LOVE   RESPECT   FAIRNESS   HONESTY

RESPONSIBILITY   KINDNESS

HONOR   BRAVERY   COMPASSION

TRUTH   HUMILITY   NONVIOLENCE

COURAGE

TOLERANCE   INTEGRITY

LOYALTY   PEACE

FREEDOM   UNITY   WISDOM   JUSTICE

THE WEALTH FORMULA	
Principle/ Lesson:	Creating financial freedom is simply a matter of developing the right habits. Interest is only interesting when I'm receiving it. Your financial habits always add up in the end.
What:	There is a formula for creating wealth and learning it early in life makes financial freedom easier than learning it later in life. Even though most of your child's Freedom Jar money won't be earning 'interest' per se (yet), the principle of compound growth (dividends buying more stock, etc.) is just one example of how your money makes you money.
Why:	The accumulation of money over time seems slow at first but then gradually speeds up due to the magic of compound interest and compound growth. It's critical that your child begin to understand that creating financial freedom is easier when he starts early. If there is one thing children have more of than their parents, it's TIME.
How:	Ask your child if he knows the formula for water. He will probably be able to tell you it's H2O. Explain that there's also a WEALTH formula and go over the three elements: time, money and interest (rate of return). Explain that the terms interest, rate of return and return on investment are often used to describe how much money your money makes. It's a bit complicated if you try to explain that interest is rate of return but rate of return is not always interest (if it's a real estate or business transaction). Leave that discussion for older kids. Just work with the concept of interest with kids ages 9-14. Ask your child to come up with examples of habits they have that are positive (e.g., doing homework, brushing their teeth, practicing a sport or musical instrument or dance, riding their horse every day, etc.). Ask them why they think it's important to make a habit of practicing. Explain there are two kinds of habits: habits people DO and habits people DON'T DO and that we're in the habit of NOT doing the habits we don't do! So, it's important to start developing positive money habits at an early age.
Comments/ Extra activities:	Share with your child your own money habits, supportive and non-supportive, and how they have affected your life, your relationships and your financial success.
Vocabulary:	Wealth formula, habits, discipline, choice, financial freedom.

Wealth Formula

Money plus Time x Interest (rate of return)

Creating financial freedom is simply a matter of developing the right habits.

What do you think this means?

_____

_____

_____

Q. Is it really true that it takes money to make money?

It's all about **Habits**!
It's all about **Discipline**!
It's all about **Choice**!

PUTTING YOUR MONEY TO WORK FOR YOU

Principle/ Lesson:	Put your money to work for you. Save Early, Save Often!
What:	Here's a little more detail about the wealth formula. The more time you have, the more money you save and invest, and the higher the interest rate or rate of return you receive, the easier and faster it is to create financial freedom.
Why:	Because investments grow exponentially over time, it's important to show your child how these three things interact to create financial freedom.
How:	Talk more about each one of the variables in depth. Ask your child what they think "Time is Money" means. Talk in terms of how much they might earn per hour and begin to equate spending also in terms of how much time they had to trade in order to have the money to buy a certain thing. Then ask them what they think the term means in terms of investing. The longer your invest your money, the more time there will be for your money to make you money.
Comments/ Extra activities:	Talk to your child about your own understanding of what this means to you. Also, talk about how owning your own business can create income to save and invest which isn't earning money per hour.
Vocabulary:	Hire, rate of return, interest, time.

© 2021 InnerWealth Publishing

It takes Time, Money and a great Rate of Return to make sure you have the money you need to support yourself when you're not able to or choose not to work anymore.

TIME:

The more TIME you have, the more money you will be able to make or earn, save and invest to meet your financial goals. SAVE EARLY, SAVE OFTEN!!!

MONEY:

The more MONEY you make and/or earn, the more money you have to save and invest to meet your financial goals.

RATE OF RETURN

The higher the RATE OF RETURN or INTEREST (%) you are making on your money, the quicker you will reach your financial goals.

Ever heard the saying...
"Time is Money?"

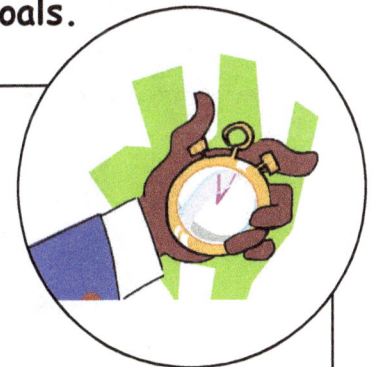

What do you think this means?

_____

_____

_____

_____

RATE OF RETURN

Principle/ Lesson:	Put your money to work for you.
What:	As explained on the last page, interest is always considered rate of return but rate of return isn't always from interest. When an asset goes up in value or appreciates in value, the resulting rate of return on investment is usually stated as a percentage. But, this isn't usually interest.
Why:	This gives your child a way to determine how hard his money is working for him. As he begins to explore the world of business, the stock market and real estate, he can begin to calculate his return on his investments and learn to make more intelligent decisions.
How:	Have your child go through the example to figure out the ROI on the widget business (explain that a widget is simply an imaginary item used in business examples). Next, have your child do the second example under 'Your Turn."
Comments/ Extra activities:	Share any stories you have about your own investments and what return on investment or interest you have received from them, both good and not so good.
Vocabulary:	Rate of return, return on investment, interest, profit, investment, widgets.

RATE OF RETURN

Your Rate of Return (also called Return on Investment or ROI) is the amount of money your money is making or returns to you when you invest it or put it to work.

It is expressed as a percentage (%) even though it may not be INTEREST that you're talking about (like on a saving account for example). It may be APPRECIATION (when the value of something you bought goes up over time so you sell it for more than you bought it for).

To figure Rate of Return, you divide the amount of money you made (buy price minus sell price) by the amount of money you invested.

EXAMPLE:

You put $100 into a little business to sell widgets. You sell your little business to your little sister a year later for $175.

- Your ROI is $75 divided by $100 or 75% ROI.
- You made 75% on your money! That's a great return!

YOUR TURN:

Let's say you bought a fancy bike for $250 and your best friend really liked it and wanted it enough to offer you $325 for it.

What is your ROI be if you sold the bike to your friend?

_____ (profit) \ _____ (investment) = _____ ROI

SIMPLE INTEREST	
Principle/ Lesson:	Interest is only interesting when you're receiving it.
What:	Parents often tell their children to 'save' part of their money but often forget to tell them why. Interest is WHY. Simple interest isn't often given on investments but is sometimes charged if a friend or relative lends you money on a short-term basis.
Why:	Explaining simple interest first makes it easier for kids to understand compound interest.
How:	Walk your child through putting $100 into a bank that pays 7% interest a year as if it were simple interest. Explain that simple interest is only paid on the original principal put into the account to begin with. Make sure to let your child know that banks don't pay anything close to 7% now but that they did many years ago. Have them call up a local bank and find out how much interest different type of accounts pay.
Comments/ Extra activities:	Come up with an example of your child lending a friend money for three months and charging the friend interest.
Vocabulary:	Principal, interest, simple interest, certificate of deposit or CD, annually, per annum, balance.

SIMPLE INTEREST

Usually (but not always anymore) when you put your money into the bank in a savings account or certificate of deposit or CD (special type of saving account where you promise not to take it out of the bank for a longer period of time) you get paid INTEREST (like a rental fee) by the bank. This is because they are using your money to loan out to other people (and they charge other people A LOT more than they are paying you).

The money you save or invest is called the PRINCIPAL. Interest is figured as a percentage (%) per year. In other words, if the interest rate is 10%, it means 10% per year (annually or per annum).

There are 2 types of interest: simple and compound.

Simple Interest = Principal x Interest Rate (%) x Time

EXAMPLE: you put $100 into your savings account which pays you 7% interest and you leave it in the account for 5 years. To calculate what the interest is (see chart below):

$100 x 7% x 5 (years) = $35.00 or

100 x .07 x 5 = 35

Simple Interest			
The interest rate is only applied to the original principal amount when computing the amount of interest.			
YEAR	PRINCIPAL	INTEREST	ENDING BALANCE
1	$100.00	$7.00	$107.00
2	$100.00	$7.00	$114.00
3	$100.00	$7.00	$121.00
4	$100.00	$7.00	$128.00
5	$100.00	$7.00	$135.00
TOTAL INTEREST			$35.00

INTERESTING INTEREST: COMPOUND

Principle/ Lesson:	Interest is only interesting when you're receiving it. The most powerful force in the universe is compound interest.
What:	Einstein was once quoted as saying, "Compound interest is the eighth wonder of the world." Compound interest is when you earn interest on your principal (money invested) AND the interest you previously made on your investment.
Why:	Because the mechanism of compound interest grows money exponentially, it's critical that kids understand how this affects their invested money over a long period of time.
How:	Walk them through the same scenario of putting $100 into an account that pays 7% interest but this time using compound interest (explaining that banks always pay compound interest). Show them how the interest (in addition to their original principal) is now also working for them. Compare the result of compound interest with simple interest in the previous example: an additional $5.26. Though this might not seem like much, ask them to multiple this by thousands or hundreds of thousands of dollars over a long period of time. The result of this is clearly evident in examples to come.
Comments/ Extra activities:	If you have an investment that pays you compound interest, show your child the statement. Get on the internet and find investment calculators so that you and your child can play with different rates of return in addition to different lengths of time (5 years, 10 years, 40 years, etc.).
Vocabulary:	Principal, interest, compound interest, compounding, balance.

Compound Interest = (Principal + Interest) x Rate (%)

Compound interest (or compounding) is even better because you earn interest on your principal AND interest. This is a GREAT thing!

EXAMPLE: You invest $100 for 5 years at an interest rate of 7% (per year). The first year you earn $7 so now your investment is worth $107.00. The second year you make 7% on the initial $100 and on the $7.00 interest you made. Now it may not seem like much extra, but over 50 years of investing it makes a HUGE difference. See below to really get the picture!

Compound Interest			
The interest rate is applied to the original principal amount AND the accumulated interest!			
YEAR	PRINCIPAL	INTEREST	ENDING BALANCE
1	$100.00	$7.00	$107.00
2	$107.00	$7.49	$114.49
3	$114.49	$8.01	$122.50
4	$122.50	$8.58	$131.08
5	$131.08	$9.18	$140.26
TOTAL INTEREST			$40.26

Which one would YOU prefer?
Simple or Compound
We thought so!

Remember, interest is only interesting when you're receiving it!

THE MAGIC OF COMPOUND INTEREST	
Principle/ Lesson:	Interest is only interesting when you're receiving it. Save Early, Save Often!
What:	This activity illustrates the power of compound interest over time and also shows how important return on investment is over time.
Why:	Because saving a little bit of money at a time seems miniscule to most kids (and adults), looking at how it compounds over a long period of time helps explain the incredible affect compound interest has on investments.
How:	Talk to the kids about how much money you, they and most adults 'waste' on piddlyjunk each week. Talk about what types of things you and they spend their money on right now. Ask them if they think they can save $10 a week for a year. Then ask them to guess how much that money would grow into if it were saved and invested each week for 50 years (put to work) at 10% and then at 12% return on investment (the average annual return of large company stocks and small company stocks respectively). The result for 10% is $756,979; the result for 12% is $1,709,453. (NOTE: these numbers vary depending on which type of calculator you use so know they are just estimates). Have your child notice the difference just 2% return made on the end result: i.e., a million dollars!
Comments/ Extra activities:	Show your child your own investment calculations in a spread sheet if you have them or show them several investment statements if you have them so they see how the money has grown (hopefully) over time. You can also show them how real estate you own has gone up in value over time or a business you started has gone up in value over time or makes more profit now that it did before.
Vocabulary:	Compound interest, piddlyjunk, stock market.

An important note about compound interest:

While most people still think that compound interest is one of the most important things to teach a child/teen, it's actually the idea of compoundING that is important for them to note.

Most financially free people do not get that way because their investment money grew using interest. It just doesn't happen now. However, there are many ways for the value of money to compound...and yes, this idea can be confusing! :-).

If you spend $10 per week on 'stuff' (piddlyjunk), can you imagine what the $10 would be worth if you started saving it instead?

$10 x 52 weeks per year = $520

If you invested that $10 a week for 50 years (from age 15-65), at the average interest rate of return for the stock market (10%), guess how much money you would have at age 65? What would you have with a 12% return on your investment?

$167,083

$1,200,000

$756,979

$26,000

$1,709,453

Write your answer here (10%): _____

Write your answer here (12%): _____

It's Magic!

THE FAMOUS RULE OF 72

Principle/ Lesson:	The higher your ROI (return on investment) or rate of return, the faster your money doubles.
What:	The Rule of 72 is simply a way to estimate how long it takes your money to double at different rates of return.
Why:	To be able to quickly calculate different rates of return in terms of how fast they will cause your investment money to double is a great tool.
How:	Ask your child how fun it would be for their money to double at some point in their life, i.e., turn $100 into $200, etc. They usually love this idea (so do most adults!). Explain that to find out how long it takes money to double at a particular interest rate or rate of return they simply take 72 and divide it by the given interest rate. The easiest example is 10% interest: 72 divided by 10 equals approximately 7.2 years. Now, have your child work through the two examples: 2% and 6%. Answer for 2% is 36 years to double and it will be worth $2000 in 36 years. Answer for 6% is 12 years to double and it will be worth $8000 in 36 years.
Comments/ Extra activities:	Go to the internet and type "investment calculators" into a search engine. Let your child put in various amounts of investment money at various rates of return to see how the amounts grow differently. Always remember to explain that the value of investments means any money they have invested in the stock market, in real estate and in businesses they own.
Vocabulary:	Rule of 72, compounding, rate of return, interest. ROI.

THE FAMOUS RULE OF 72

The number of years it takes your money to double.

72 ÷ Interest Rate = # years to double

"Compounding is the 8th wonder of the world." - Albert Einstein

Imagine you've saved $1000! (YES, you CAN do this). Let's see how long it takes to double your money at different rates of return...

NOTE: Remember, **generally**, the higher the ROI (return on investment) you get, the higher the risk associated with that investment. This is why it's so important to learn how to make educated investment decisions and to manage risk (not avoid it).

If you're getting a **2% return** (72 divided by 2 = 36)

Number of years to double? _____

What will your investment be worth in 36 years? _____

How about a **6% return** (72 divided by 6 = _____)

Number of years to double? _____

What will your investment be worth in 36 years? _____

As ROI/interest rate goes up, the number of years it takes your money to double goes down.

GROWING YOUR MONEY	
Principle/ Lesson:	Invest your money wisely. Put your money to work for you.
What:	This chart illustrates why it's important to research how much interest or the rate of return you are getting on any investment, and keep in mind that interest rates and ROI can change over the lifetime of any investment. A small percentage increase (or decrease) in the interest rate can make a huge difference in the end result over the lifetime of an investment.
Why:	Seeing how different interest rates affect the end result of an investment will help motivate your child to find the best investments possible as an adult (hopefully).
How:	Have your child pick an interest rate and then walk through the chart as the investment ages from 1 year to 50. Then, multiple the result of $1 by $1000 and then $10,000 and finally $100,000. For example, $10,000 as an initial investment, will, at a 15% rate of return over 40 years, grow to $2,678,600!
Comments/ Extra activities:	Give your child personal examples if you have them.
Vocabulary:	Growth rates, compound interest rate, risk.

HOW $1 GROWS OVER TIME

Growth Rates (Compound Interest Rate)

YEARS	3%	5%	7%	9%	11%	15%
1	1.03	1.05	1.07	1.09	1.11	1.15
5	1.16	1.28	1.40	1.54	1.69	2.01
10	1.34	1.63	1.97	2.37	2.64	4.05
15	1.56	2.08	2.76	3.64	4.78	8.14
20	1.81	2.65	3.87	5.60	8.06	16.37
25	2.09	3.39	5.43	8.62	13.59	32.92
30	2.43	4.32	7.61	13.27	22.89	66.21
35	2.81	5.52	10.68	20.41	38.57	133.18
40	3.26	7.04	14.97	31.41	65.00	267.86
45	3.78	8.99	21.00	48.33	109.56	538.77
50	4.38	11.46	29.46	74.36	184.56	1083.66

Keep in mind that interest rates are rarely stable but are averaged out over a period of time. Also remember that a higher rate of return usually (but not always) means higher risk.

LEVERAGE: A MAJOR KEY TO BUILDING WEALTH	
Principle/ Lesson:	Learning to use leverage is how most people create wealth.
What:	Leverage is utilizing other people's time, energy and money to make you money. It's also defined as the use of borrowed money to increase investing power. You use leverage in a business when you hire employees to work for you so they make more money for your business than you can make alone. You also are using leverage in your business when you borrow money to expand the business. You use leverage in real estate when you buy a $100,000 property by borrowing $80,000 from the bank and using only $20,000 of your own money and also when you buy an investment property and have a tenant (renter) paying your mortgage each month. Note: The idea of leverage can be applied to stock market type investments, however, these strategies are quite risky.
Why:	It's important to get children to start thinking in terms of working smarter instead of harder. People with lots of money don't do everything themselves; they hire people to do work for them.
How:	Ask your child how he would lift an elephant. Look at the diagram on the page that shows using a heavy object on one side to lift the elephant. Set up a physical form of a lever system where he has to lift something that is too heavy to lift by himself, but with the help of a pole propped on top of a box or rock, he could lift it easily. Ask him to think about a teeter-totter in a playground and see if he can explain why a heavy person can balance with a lighter person. Since we've already explored Financial Fourscore and the idea of having employees, he should have an initial idea of what leverage is.
Comments/ Extra activities:	Ask your child how he might use leverage to make money now and in the future. Share experiences you have had with your child that have involved using leverage to make you money. Note: We refer to the stock market, real estate and building business enterprises as the Three Pillars of Wealth.
Vocabulary:	Leverage, lever, real estate, business, stocks, mutual funds.

LEVERAGE: A MAJOR KEY TO BUILDING WEALTH

Leverage:

If you wanted to lift an elephant by yourself, how would you do it?

You'd use a **LEVER**.

A lever is a tool that gives you the advantage of being several people at the same time. Financial freedom comes from using leverage to your advantage.

Leverage is utilizing Other People's Time, Energy or Money to make YOU money. Borrowing money from a bank to buy real estate, borrowing money to expand your business or hire employees to make money for the business are common examples of using leverage to build financial freedom.

So, could you lift an elephant all by yourself?

Yes, as long as you had the right tools and those tools are?

        Other people's _____

        Other people's _____

        Other people's _____

MANAGE RISK WITH DIVERSIFICATION, ASSET ALLOCATION

Principle/ Lesson:	You need to learn how to manage risk, not avoid it. Don't put all your financial eggs in one basket.
What:	Everything in life has risks attached to it; driving, flying, playing sports, trying new things, relationships, etc. However, there is usually a direct correlation between the potential reward (return on investment) of an investment and the risk for that investment. Diversification is when you more than one investment in the same area of investing. In other words, buy several different banking stocks or several rental properties. On the other hand, there is also the concept of Asset Allocation. This refers to the idea that you spread your investment money over several different 'types' of investment assets, i.e., some in real estate, some in a business and some in the stock market.
Why:	Teaching your child to be responsible for learning as much as possible about each investment he makes will help him reduce the risks associated with investing.
How:	First, have your child look up the word 'diversification' in the glossary or in a dictionary. Ask your child what might happen to his body if he only ate one food for a year (he'd probably become malnourished). Ask your child if he can name a few activities that don't include at least a little risk. Explain that investing is the same; it has risks, but he can reduce his risk by researching investments and also by putting his money into many different types of investments, i.e., some in the stock market, some in real estate and some into a business. The other way investors reduce their risks when investing is to develop investing systems for whatever type of investing they choose to do.
Comments/ Extra activities:	Explain how you or someone you know has diversified. Watch for examples of people who lose everything because they've invested all of their money in one thing.
Vocabulary:	Risk, return, diversification, research, risk-return triangle.

There is often a direct connection between risk and your Return on Investment (or interest) that you get from your investments. Generally, the higher the potential return, the greater the risk.

See the Risk/Return Triangle below...

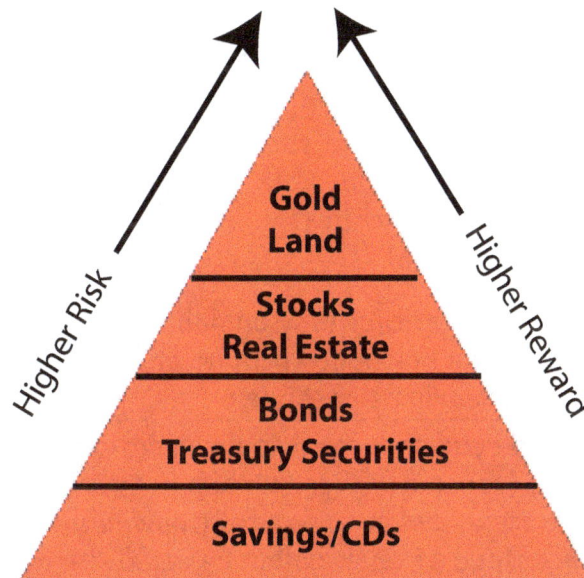

Investments make money two ways:
Income & Appreciation

It's very important to understand what type of investments you're putting your money into and the risk that's associated with those investments.

Investing without doing your research and having a system is like gambling! You wouldn't want to gamble with your future, don't do it with your money either.

It's YOUR responsibility to make sure your money is invested wisely!

DIVERSIFICATION AND ASSET ALLOCATION HELP REDUCE

INVESTMENT RISK AND INCREASE RETURN.

PAY YOURSELF FIRST	
Principle/ Lesson:	Pay Yourself First. Save Early, Save Often.
What:	Pay Yourself First is one of the oldest, and most important, wealth principles known to man. It means you save a portion of every dollar you earn/make and invest it wisely. If you don't develop this habit, chances are you will never accumulate much wealth or create a stream of money to live on when you are older. This is sometimes called Retirement Income. It's estimated that about 20% of the American population inherits their wealth. However, if those people never learn how to manage that money, they often end up losing it over time.
Why:	It's important for your child to start practicing the habit of 'paying yourself first' as soon as possible. We encourage you to embrace the Ultimate Allowance* concept if you're not already providing some type of an allowance to your child. Most children also get birthday or holiday money, gifts from relatives, odd jobs around the house or from neighbors, so it's great to get them into this habit as early as possible.
How:	Have your child read through the information and walk him through the A-B-C process (pages 36-37). Ask him if there's a new habit he'd like to create and make a plan to put that new habit into practice, including saving a percentage of each dollar he receives, regardless of how he receive it.
Comments/ Extra activities:	If your child doesn't have a savings account yet, please start one ASAP. Based on The Money Jars (pages 70-753), decide how much of his income to put into each jar (living, freedom, savings, education, play, donation). Once your child has saved up $50 in the Saving Jar, start separate savings accounts for the different jars and have the bank label each account with the names of the jars. (You may have to call around to find a bank or credit union that will do this, AND watch out for fees). When the statements arrive each month (or is ready to be printed online), put a slip of paper with the jar total in each jar. If you're used to using Excel, feel free to develop an Excel sheet for each jar as well. Help your child create file folders for each account to file the statements in. Great financial habits developed at a young age yield great financial returns later in life. GREAT BOOK: Richest Man in Babylon by George Clason
Vocabulary:	Savings account, checking account, expenses.

* The Ultimate Allowance Book is available at www.FinancialEducationStore.com & Amazon.

PAY YOURSELF FIRST

Pay Yourself First is THE SINGLE MOST important money habit you can learn! If YOU don't start saving your money so you can start to invest it, no one else is going to do it for you, so start now! The first step for most people is developing the SAVING HABIT.

First, you need to save up a little money at home in a piggy bank, wallet, jar, old sock or drawer.

Then have your parents take you to the bank to start your first **Savings Account!**

Every time you get money, whether it's from a gift, birthday or job, take a portion of the money and 'save it' in your new savings account.

You'll be amazed at how quickly your new account will begin to add up and the faster it adds up, the more you want to save!

But what about a Checking Account?

When you start paying for many of your own expenses (clothes, music, sports, entertainment, lessons, etc.), you can open a CHECKING ACCOUNT. This way you won't mix your Spending Jar money with your Saving and Freedom Jar money.

INVESTMENTS – THE THREE PILLARS OF WEALTH

Principle/ Lesson:	Put your money to work for you. Assets Feed You, Liabilities Eat You
What:	Introducing the terms Investing and Investment at a young age gives kids a great way to look at the choices they make with their money. Understanding the idea and process of 'investing' money, as well as what a good investment looks like, is critical for your child's long-term financial stability. Investment: Technically, you can invest your time, your energy and/or your money into something called an asset that either grows in value, called appreciation, creates/produces cash flow or passive income or preferably, BOTH! The classic types of assets people use to create appreciation and/or passive income are what we call The Three Pillars of Wealth: • Real Estate • Business • Stock Market The word Investing refers to the ACT of putting money into an investment. More on the types of investments in a bit.
Why:	Investing is how human beings create money to support themselves when they don't want to or can't work anymore for money. This can happen at any age. Note: This section on investing may be challenging if you, the parent or guardian, isn't educated in investing yourself, but the good news is that you're going to learn right along with your child! This is a good thing!
How:	First, download and read the story of The Golden Goose to your child if they've never heard it before. It's a good idea to revisit the story even if they have. Talk about what Pillars are used for when building a house...i.e., to make it stable. Investing in at least two of the three pillars of wealth is how people develop financial stability. If one area struggles or loses money, the other one or two usually maintain value. Explore the many ways you can invest in The Three Pillars of Wealth.
Comments/ Extra Activities:	See the next page for all the different types of investments that the three pillars represent.
Vocabulary:	Investing, assets, cash flow, passive income, growth, appreciation, golden goose, golden eggs.

THE THREE PILLARS OF WEALTH

When you INVEST your money in ASSETS, you are creating a Golden Goose who lays Golden Eggs (money) for you to live on when you decide you don't want to work anymore or can't work anymore.

Once you have created your Golden Goose and have it laying Golden Eggs, you NEVER, NEVER, NEVER want to kill it (i.e., spend it)

Real Estate

Appreciation and/or Cash Flow (rental income)

Business

Appreciation and/or Cash Flow (profits)

Stock Market

Appreciation and/or Cash Flow (dividends & interest)

Your <u>Foundation</u> for Financial Freedom!

THE THREE PILLARS OF WEALTH ASSETS

Principle/ Lesson:	Put your money to work for you. Assets feed you, Liabilities eat you. There are as many ways to invest as there are people.
What:	There are many, MANY types of investments and investment strategies that people use to become financially free. The way you learn what you want to invest in is to notice which ones are of interest to you and which ones are easiest to learn for you. There are literally thousands of educational programs that teach about different types of investment strategies.
Why:	Investing can be confusing for people...usually because of lack of knowledge. Just knowing what types of investments exist in the world gives children ideas about what they may want to learn as they get older and have saved up money to invest.
How:	Go over the different types of Assets and open up a conversation with your child about them. If you and/or any of your adult friends own any of these, invite them over to talk to your child about the advantages and disadvantages of the different types of investments. Do some research on the web about the different types of investments to see which ones spark your child's interest. Encourage them to learn more.
Comments/ Extra activities:	If you see your child more interested in one type of investment than another, order a few books on the topic. Either read them together or pay your child to read the books and only pay them after they give you a book report and have a conversation about what they learned and how they can use the information now and in the future.
Vocabulary:	Real estate, business, stock market, flipping houses, stocks, bonds, ETFs, mutual funds, service business, retail business, wholesale business, FOREX, dividend, mutual funds, block chain, REIT.

THREE PILLARS OF WEALTH ASSETS

REAL ESTATE

BUSINESS

STOCK MARKET

REAL ESTATE	BUSINESS	STOCK MARKET
House You Live In	Retail Store	Individual Stocks
House You Rent Out	Online Business	Bonds (loan investments)
Flipping Real Estate (buying to fix up and sell for a profit)	Wholesale Store	Mutual Funds
Housing Development	Coffee House	ETFs (Exchange Traded Funds)
School Building	Restaurant	Dividend Producing Stocks or Funds
Hospital/Medical Building	Service Business like plumbing, electrical, etc.	REITS (Real Estate Investment Trusts)
Apartment Building	Service Business like lawyer, accountant, etc.	FOREX (buying and selling of currencies)
Business Building	Medical Business	Block chain Technologies like Bitcoin
Mall Building	Fitness Gym or Club	
Storage facility	Sports Team	
Parking Lot	Investment Business	
Farm Land		
Land You Think Will Increase in Value		

BANKS AND YOUR MONEY

Principle/ Lesson:	Put your money to work for you. Save early, save often.
What:	Banks are generally in the business of making money by LENDING/ LOANING money to people and businesses. They make money by charging INTEREST to the people/businesses who BORROW money. Banks loan money for all sorts of things: • Real Estate (houses, rental property, shopping malls, stores) • Business (start up business, expanding a business) • Automobiles (cars, trucks, etc.) • Boats • Personal Loans (to be used for medical and other personal projects) Looking at investments in terms of whether you are 'lending' your money in exchange for interest or purchasing something to 'own' that brings you appreciation (increase in value) and cash flow, is necessary when evaluating investment options.
Why:	Certain types of investments carry higher potential risk but also bring higher potential reward. It's important to understand the different risks associated with different types of investments.
How:	Talk to your child about what happens when they put their money into a bank, i.e., you are LENDING your money to the bank in exchange for a little bit of interest (rental fee) although not all banks pay interest anymore. The bank then lends YOUR money (along with lots of other people's money) to other people and businesses to buy houses, cars, boats, etc., and to start and expand businesses and they lend this money out at a higher rate of interest than it is paying you. The bank makes money by charging a higher percentage of interest on the loans than what they pay you in interest. They often also charge FEES to people who are taking out loans from them. These FEES are often called POINTS and are usually a percentage of the loan amount. In other words, they might charge "five points" (i.e., 5%) on a loan.
Comments/ Extra activities:	Discuss your own current investment accounts and other investments and discuss whether they are LOAN or OWNERSHIP investments.
Vocabulary:	Loan investment, ownership investment, profits, rental income, dividends, rate of return, risk, CDs, money market accounts, stock mutual funds, collectibles, bonds.

BANKS AND YOUR MONEY

Q. What is a Loan Investment?

When you put your money into a bank account (checking, savings, CDs, money markets), you are Lending your money to the bank. The bank then pays you interest to use your money to loan out to people and businesses and charges them more interest than it's paying you (that's how banks make money). These are called Loan Investments as opposed to Ownership Investments.

Q. What is an Ownership Investment?

An investment in an asset that you own (see below). This type of investment makes money through appreciation of the asset, rental income, profits or dividends.

Q. Are Loan Investments or Ownership Investments risky?

Loan Investments normally have a guaranteed rate of return (interest rate) and are considered low risk.

Ownership Investments don't have a guaranteed rate of return and the risks can vary depending on the asset.

* LOAN * INVESTMENTS	* OWNERSHIP * INVESTMENTS
Savings Accounts	Starting a Business
Checking Accounts	Stocks
Certificates of Deposits (CD)	Mutual Funds
Money Market Accounts	EFTs
Bonds	Real Estate
	Rental Property
	Collectibles

SAVING VS. INVESTING

Principle/ Lesson:	Saving is short-term, Investing is generally long-term.
What:	There are major differences between why and where you 'save' your money and why and where you 'invest' your money. Saving is a short-term, low reward (low risk) method to save up money to buy things, use as contingency money or use as investing into an asset. Investing accounts are medium to long-term, usually higher risk (higher reward) and used to put your money to work for your future. Liquidity refers to how quickly you can turn your account into cash if you need it.
Why:	It's important to know what type of account to open for what purpose.
How:	Read through the two tables discussing each topic.
Comments/ Extra activities:	Share with your child the different types of accounts you have. NOTE: We use the word 'contingency' instead of 'emergency.' We figure that if you plan for an emergency, you may just get one.
Vocabulary:	Saving, investing, liquidity, ROI (return on investment), safety.

SAVING VS. INVESTING

SAVING

Time frame:	Short
Risk:	Very little
Objective:	Contingency Fund
	Large purchase
Type:	Savings account
	Money Market
	CD
Liquidity:	Very liquid
ROI:	Low
Safe:	Usually

INVESTING

Time frame:	Med to long
Risk:	Low to high
Objective:	Retirement
	Freedom Acct
Type:	Mutual Funds
	Stocks (Equity)
	Real Estate
	Business
Liquidity:	Depends
ROI:	Low to high
Guaranteed:	Not usually

The Best Way to Double Your Money is to Fold it in Half and Put it in Your Pocket!

While this is a humorous saying, the best way to double your money is to invest it wisely.

INVESTMENT AND RETIREMENT ACCOUNTS

Principle/ Lesson:	Get taxes out of the picture when you can. Use tax rules to your advantage.
What:	Investment accounts are accounts where you typically deposit your money that's then invested in stocks, ETFs, mutual funds and bonds. While it's beyond the scope of this program, it's important to understand what types of investments provide interest vs. dividend income. Generally speaking, savings accounts, money market accounts, bonds and parts of mutual funds can produce some interest income as well as dividend income, depending on the actual investment. The interest and dividend income is two potential sources of the cash flow necessary to financial freedom. Taxes, as we'll discuss, take a large chunk out of most people's paychecks so it's important to understand ways to invest that protect the money you're investing. Certain types of investment/retirement accounts can provide tax advantages although there are financially free people who never invest in these types of accounts. Again, it requires education to learn about all of the options.
Why:	The US government has created the opportunity to put money away for our futures in special accounts that allow us to reduce or eliminate in some case, paying large amounts of tax on our investment money. Those accounts, called IRAs, 401Ks (and other names), allow us to put money away and deduct that amount from our current taxable income in most cases. Since kids are just starting to save for their futures, they need to know WHERE to start saving and investing. Since most people don't become investment experts, hiring a professional to help you decide which type of investment account is best for you is very important.
How:	Read through this page letting your child ask questions that come up. If your child doesn't know the story of the Golden Goose (Aesop Fable), look it up or tell it to him if you know it. Explain that as investment accounts grow, they produce golden eggs (interest and dividends) and that's what you live off of when you decide to stop working for money.
Comments/ Extra activities:	Tell your child what types of accounts you currently have, how much you're contributing, what type of return you're getting, etc. Show him your monthly statements and teach him how to read it and then show him each month as they arrive in the mail (or via the web).
Vocabulary:	Investment accounts, golden goose, retirement accounts, IRA, taxes, brokerage company, stocks, mutual funds, bonds.

Investment Accounts

are accounts where you put your money to grow for the future and for retirement.

Money in these accounts is usually invested in stocks, EFT's, mutual funds and bonds.

> ## * Investment Accounts *
>
> **Banks · Brokerage Businesses**
>
> **Online (internet) Businesses**
>
> **Insurance Companies**

They are your Golden Goose Accounts and will produce income for you when you stop working.

Retirement Accounts

are special types of Investment Accounts that offer great tax advantages. They have special rules and, depending on the type of account, can have penalties (fees) if you take the money out before you're supposed to.

Retirement Accounts have funny names...a 401(k) account is available at your job (it's called a 403(b) if it's a nonprofit organization); a Tradition IRA or Roth IRA (individual retirement account) is available at any brokerage company like American Express, Morgan Stanley, Edward Jones, TD-Ameritrade and Etrade.com, your bank, or other financial business.

Some retirement accounts are for employees, others for self-employed.

> ## * Retirement Accounts *
>
> **401K · 403B · Roth IRA**
>
> **Traditional IRA · Sep IRA**

There's NO RULE that says you have to be OLD to retire.

What age do you want to be financially free? _____

PUTTING YOUR MONEY TO WORK FOR YOU

Principle/ Lesson:	Assets feed you; liabilities eat you. Put your money to work for you.
What:	Assets are the cornerstones of your financial freedom portfolio (total package of investments). Assets do two things: grow (go up) in value and produce passive income that goes IN your pocket. Liabilities are debts you OWE to others and they take money OUT of your pocket. As we've mentioned before, a liability that allows you to invest in an asset that produces enough money (cash flow/profit) to pay the monthly payment of the liability is called good debt. Even more importantly, every dollar you spend on piddlyjunk (instead of investing in an asset that will grow) increases the time it takes you to become financially free. You get one chance to choose to put each dollar you earn or make to work for you or waste its potential by buying piddlyjunk.
Why:	It's important to understand what assets and liabilities are and why assets are the key to creating financial freedom.
How:	Have your child read the definition of an asset and a liability. Ask them if they can name a few of each. You'll probably have to help. Assets: stocks, real estate, business (especially an automated internet business), taxi, car (if it's a collectible car that will grow in value), boat (if used for a business), gold, silver, coins, rare collectibles. Liabilities: cars (personal), clothing, piddlyjunk, trinkets, boats (pleasure), house you live in (note explanation earlier on houses as assets vs. liabilities), stereos, games, sports equipment, computers, etc.
Comments/ Extra activities:	Have your child go around the house and name assets and liabilities. Virtually everything in your house will probably be a liability that is not making you money. If someone in the family uses a van or truck for work and has tools they use to make money, those are assets also in a way. If a member of the family makes money on the internet, discuss the fact that the computer they use is an asset because it makes them money.
Vocabulary:	Assets, liabilities, ownership, guaranteed, risks, return, portfolio.

Assets & Liabilities:

Once you have a little money saved up, you are ready to make your first investment, in other words, buy your first asset. Assets are things that have value and generally, you OWN them. You know you have an asset when it brings you cash flow, it grows in value, or both!

Most people, however, spend their money on piddlyjunk or things that turn into LIABILITIES. You know you have a liability if it costs you money to keep or maintain or it loses value over time.

List a few assets and liabilities here...

ASSETS
(feed you)

_____

_____

_____

_____

_____

_____

_____

LIABILITIES
(eat you)

_____

_____

_____

_____

_____

_____

_____

The Return on Investment (the amount of money your money makes for you) on an Ownership Investments is NOT guaranteed and the risks are usually higher, however, the return may also be higher.

HOW YOUR MONEY MAKES MONEY FOR YOU

Principle/ Lesson:	Put your money to work for you. Assets feed you.
What:	There are three primary ways that people become financially free: • They invest in the stock market • They invest real estate • They start or invest in a business. We call these "the three pillars of wealth" because they are the three most common ways people create enough regular (monthly) passive income so they don't have to go to work at a job anymore unless they want to. Many financially free people invest in more than one type.
Why:	Learning the concept of why and how to create enough passive income (cash flow) to cover your monthly expenses in order to stop working for money helps your child begin to think about financial choices in this context. Most adults don't think in these terms; they simply continue to increase their monthly expenses and put in hour after hour working to pay for their 'stuff' and never consider the long-term financial consequences/ramifications/requirements of their choices. By teaching a child how passive income is created, they can make wiser choices from the very beginning of their investment career.
How:	Ask your child to think about people he knows that are financially free, don't work at a job anymore, etc. Ask them if they have heard any of these people talk about how they've 'made' their money. See if they can name the three pillars: stocks, real estate and business. Once you've helped them uncover these three types of investments, see if they can guess how the investment makes the investor money. Go over the details on the next page, illustrating with personal examples.
Comments/ Extra activities:	Using a newspaper, or the internet, do some research and find stories about companies whose stock has gone up over time, find local and national news about how the values of real estate go up and down and finally, how someone has started and sold a business for a profit. While this is actually 'appreciation' at work, it shows them how they make money two ways with assets: appreciation and cash flow.
Vocabulary:	Appreciation, stocks, mutual funds, rental property, dividend, profit, interest income, passive income.

HOW YOUR MONEY MAKES MONEY FOR YOU

Your money makes you money in two basic ways:

1) When your asset or investment goes up in value so you can sell it for more than you bought it for (called APPRECIATION):

   a) Stock, ETFs, mutual funds, bonds

   b) Real estate

   c) A business

AND/OR

2) When assets or investments create PASSIVE INCOME (also called CASH FLOW OR POSITIVE CASH FLOW):

   a) Interest income from savings accounts, CDs, money market accounts, bonds

   b) Rental income from real estate you rent to people or businesses

   c) Dividend income from stocks (dividends are business profits)

   d) Profit from a business, online or brick and mortar

START NOW, DON'T WAIT	
Principle/ Lesson:	Save Early, Save Often.
What:	Starting early is the single most important key to accumulating wealth. With times comes enough education and the establishment of financial habits that make all the difference.
Why:	Because of the concept of compounding interest and the fact that investments grow exponentially over a long period of time, investing while you are young almost guarantees you financial freedom at a relatively early age (compared to many who retire at 65-70). Note: this concept involves the ACCUMULATION of money and the growth of that accumulation over time, not the UTILIZATION of money and regular cash flow you create from investing in dividend producing stocks, rental income from real estate, profits from businesses.
How:	First, ask your child at what age he would like to stop working? Ask him why just to get an idea what he thinks about retirement. It's interesting what children glean from listening to adults about retirement. Many active adults don't ever consider retirement an option until they just get tired of doing what they're doing one day. There are truly no rules. Show your child how much money he'd have to save if he had 40 years to accumulate $1 million. Then move down the chart to having 35 years and then so on. When you get to having 20 years and less left before you want to retire, the amount that has to be invested each month gets bigger and bigger, posing a bigger and bigger challenge for people who haven't started saving and investing for retirement. Ask your child if he understands why it's so important, and so much easier, to start saving and investing when he's young.
Comments/ Extra activities:	Note about rate of return being 10%. While it's virtually impossible to achieve a 10% return on money saved in a bank, there are many ways to invest money in order to get a 10% return or even greater. The key is to spend part of your Education Jar learning how to invest your money! Talk to your kids about your own investing strategies, your successes, your mistakes, things you would have changed had you learned how money worked earlier (if you didn't), etc.
Vocabulary:	Retirement, exponentially (look up in order to explain).

When it comes to having more than enough money than you need when you want to stop working, TIME can be your worst enemy or your greatest friend. Regardless of your age, the rule of thumb is:

START NOW!

Let's say you want to have $1,000,000 at retirement. Look what you must save every month, depending on your age, if you're getting a 10% rate of return.

Years to Retirement		Monthly Investment Needed
40	$$	$158 per month
35	$$$	$263 per month
30	$$$$$	$442 per month
25	$$$$$$$	$754 per month
20	$$$$$$$$$$	$1,317 per month
15	$$$$$$$$$$$	$2,412 per month
10	$$$$$$$$$$$$$	$4,881 per month
5	$$$$$$$$$$$$$$	$12,931 per month!!!

Don't Wait!
Put Time on YOUR Side!

THE TEST OF TIME	
Principle/ Lesson:	Save Early, Save Often Put your money to work for you. Put your money to work for you.
What:	Saving and investing money early and often is better than saving and investing money later. It's much easier to create a lot of wealth when you start earlier because the money has more TIME to grow!
Why:	The growth of money saved at an earlier age grows into larger sums at retirement because of the effect of compounding growth and the simple fact that investments have a longer time to increase in value.
How:	Look at the two different scenarios focusing on the total amount of money invested for each scenario and how much was accumulated: Person A - Invested $24,000 total, from age 19 to 26, and ended up with $964,129 Person B - Invested $102,000 total, but didn't start until age 27 and invested until age 60, and ended up with $810,073 Ask which Person they would prefer to be. Ask what the most significant difference is between the two scenarios and let them know the biggest advantage they have over any adult is TIME.
Comments/ Extra activities:	Again, share your own investing experiences with your child. If you're able, do examples with different amounts invested and also different rates of return.
Vocabulary:	Tax-deferred, IRA, Roth IRA, 401K.

Person A opens a TAX-DEFERRED ACCOUNT (IRA, Roth IRA, 401K) and invests $3000 a year for 8 years starting at age 19 and then stops investing at age 26. Total investments average a 10% return.

Person B spends (instead of invests) $3000 for 8 years, then decides to open a TAX-DEFERRED ACCOUNT and invests $3000 a year for the next 34 years which also averages a 10% return.

PERSON A

age	payment	year end	age	payment	year end
19	$3000	3,300	42		173,407
20	$3000	6,930	43		190,748
21	$3000	10,923	44		209,823
22	$3000	15,315	45		230,805
23	$3000	20,147	46		253,885
24	$3000	25,462	47		279,274
25	$3000	31,308	48		307,201
26	$3000	37,738	49		337,921
27		41,512	50		371,712
28		45,663	51		408,885
29		50,230	52		449,773
30		55,253	53		494,751
31		60,778	54		544,227
32		66,856	55		598,648
33		73,542	56		658,513
34		80,896	57		724,364
35		88,985	58		796,801
36		97,883	59		876,480
37		107,672	60		964,129
38		118,439			
39		130,283			
40		143,312			
41		157,643			

Invested $24,000
Grand Total $964,129

PERSON B

age	payment	year end	age	payment	year end
19		0	42	$3000	118,634
20		0	43	$3000	133,798
21		0	44	$3000	150,477
22		0	45	$3000	168,825
23		0	46	$3000	189,008
24		0	47	$3000	211,208
25		0	48	$3000	235,629
26		0	49	$3000	262,492
27	$3000	3,300	50	$3000	292,041
28	$3000	6,930	51	$3000	324,545
29	$3000	10,923	52	$3000	360,300
30	$3000	15,315	53	$3000	399,630
31	$3000	20,147	54	$3000	442,893
32	$3000	25,462	55	$3000	490,482
33	$3000	31,308	56	$3000	542,830
34	$3000	37,738	57	$3000	600,413
35	$3000	44,812	58	$3000	663,755
36	$3000	52,593	59	$3000	733,430
37	$3000	61,153	60	$3000	810,073
38	$3000	70,568			
39	$3000	80,924			
40	$3000	92,317			
41	$3000	104,849			

Invested $102,000
Ended up with $810,073

Save Early, Save Often!

When should YOU start saving and investing? _____

TAXES AND INFLATION: WEALTH'S ENEMIES

Principle/ Lesson:	The golden rule: he who has the gold makes the rules. The 'other' golden rule: the rules apply to everyone. Entrepreneurs and investors often pay less in taxes than employees.
What:	Taxes takes a huge bite out of our money's potential to grow. Though taxes pay for great things (see list), it's important to know the tax laws so you can take advantage of them. They were created for everyone so it's up to everyone to learn the rules that work best for them. Inflation means that the cost of things go up over time. The average inflation rate in the US changes every year but a good estimate is 3% per year. There are many conflicting ideas about our inflation rate in the US. Understanding inflation shows your child that his investments need to make over 3% return on investment (ROI) just to maintain his money's buying power. Joke: "Inflation is when you pay fifteen dollars for the ten-dollar haircut you used to get for five dollars when you had hair." --Sam Ewing
Why:	Explore with your child the things taxes pay for (roads, police, etc.) and then look at all the different types of taxes we pay. A small difference in interest rate or rate of return results in a huge difference over a long period of time. Letting large sums of money sit in a saving account that makes less than 3% interest actually COSTS you money. Children need to understand how inflation affects the economy and vice versa. Understanding how taxes and inflation influence investment growth is critical when working toward financial freedom. It can make a tremendous difference in the time it takes to reach financial goals.
How:	Simply read through the page. Use the example of doubling a dollar 20 times tax-free (no taxes taken out) at the top of the page vs. doubling a dollar but getting taxes taken out each time it doubles. Ask why taxes are such a big enemy to wealth creation and how they can avoid it. NOTE: We don't advocate tax evasion of any sort, but simply being aware of the impact of taxes and inflation and the current tax laws will help your child build and keep his wealth.
Comments/ Extra activities:	Look at a few of your utility bills with your child so they can see that there are taxes involved in just about everything we do.
Vocabulary:	Taxes, inflation, government.

> Double a dollar 20 times,
> without taxes = $1,048,567
>
> Double a dollar 20 times,
> but deduct 33% income tax each time you
> double it = $28,466

DID YOU KNOW: On average, you work nearly half the year for the Government!

It's important to understand our tax laws

so you pay only what you have to pay.

Other taxes we pay:

• Federal income tax • State income tax • Sales tax • Gasoline tax • Liquor tax • Hotel tax • Cigarette tax • Telephone tax • Cable tax • Utility tax • and a lot more!

INFLATION

Inflation is when the cost of goods and services goes up over time. The inflation rate in the U.S. changes every year but has averaged about 3% per year.

If something costs $1 today, what will it cost next year with a 3% inflation rate?_____ (hint: $1 x 1.03 = _____)

If you put a dollar under your bed today, what's it worth next year? _____ (hint: $1 − ($1 x .03) = _____)

PASSIVE INCOME & THE THREE PILLARS OF WEALTH

Principle/ Lesson:	To create financial freedom, invest your money wisely. Asset feeds you, Liabilities eat you. Make money grow by putting it to work for you.
What:	This is a review of the Three Pillars of Wealth because learning the concept of investing in assets is the key to financial freedom. Assets feed you by increasing in value and producing regular passive income to live on when you're not working or trading your time and energy for money. Passive income is income you don't have to work for (or rather, GO to work for). When you stop working for a living at a job, you need to replace that income with other income in order to pay for the lifestyle of your choice. By investing in assets that produce regular cash flow/passive income, you continue making money to live on.
Why:	It's important to understand that creating financial freedom is not just about getting a job and saving up enough money to live on when you're older. This strategy takes decades to accomplish because you're not putting your money to work for you. The money you save must be invested wisely in assets that produce cash flow to live on and hopefully go up in value over the long run.
How:	Explain that most financially free people normally invest in at least two, or all three, of these types of assets to build their wealth and create cash flow to live on. All three can appreciate over time (go up in value) and all three can produce cash flow to live on, which is more important for creating financial freedom than the asset appreciating. Discuss rental income for rental property, i.e., the fact that your renter is paying your house loan/mortgage for you. Talk about the profits in a business, i.e., you sell things for more than you buy or make them for or provide a service that people pay for. Talk about how stocks can pay dividends, i.e., portion of the profits given to stockholders but note that not all stocks pay dividends.
Comments/ Extra activities:	Talk to a friend who is a realtor or better yet, find someone who is a real estate investor who can share his/her experience with your child. Do the same for someone who owns a profitable business and invests in stocks, REITS, ETFs or mutual funds.
Vocabulary:	Assets, real estate, cash flow, rental income, appreciation, profits, dividends.

Let's review how these assets create income you can live on when you don't want to go to work anymore.

Real Estate

Business

Stock Market

Real Estate	Business	Stock Market
Rental income *Appreciation*	*Profits* *Monthly revenue streams* *Appreciation*	*Dividends* *Interest* *Appreciation*

How will YOU create Passive Income to live on?

PERSONAL FINANCIAL STATEMENT

Principle/ Lesson:	To keep your money on track, keep track of your money. People don't plan to fail, they fail to plan. Your financial habits always add up in the end.
What:	A personal financial statement is your adult financial report card. It is a snapshot of your financial situation on any given day and it changes from day to day, month to month, and year to year. It also lets a lender or banker (someone who is going to lend you money to buy something) know if you have enough assets (aka net worth) to cover the loan in case for some reason you can't make the payments. Your Net Worth is what you OWN minus what you OWE and gives you a baseline from which to make financial decisions.
Why:	Unless you keep constant track of how well you are doing financially, you won't know when to change investments, when to invest more money, when to sell investments, etc. In terms of getting a loan, your lender/banker doesn't care what grade you got in English or Math in high school or college. He DOES care how well you've done financially though: • How much you've saved. • How much you have invested. • What you own. • How well you pay your bills. • How high your credit score is.
How:	The best way to use this page with your child is to use your own financial situation, letting your child fill in the page with real figures. If you don't want to do that for some reason, help him come up with some reasonable figures and let him figure out the net worth. Remember that the second key to raising money savvy adults is to involve them in everything money related at home. Kids don't mind that you don't have it all together. It helps them feel OK about not being perfect.
Comments/ Extra activities:	Let your child see your last financial statement and if you don't have one, let him help you create one. It's a great activity for the whole family.
Vocabulary:	Personal financial statement, assets, liabilities, current value, net worth.

Your Adult Report Card!

Assets	Current Value ($)
Cash in Savings Account	_____
Cash in Checking Account	_____
Money in retirement accounts	_____
Money people owe you (called receivables)	_____
Real Estate Owned	_____
Automobiles (value)	_____
Personal Property (value)	_____
Stock Owned	_____
Bonds Owned	_____
Mutual Funds/EFTs Owned	_____
Other Assets (collectibles)	_____
Total Assets	$_____

Liabilities	Current Value ($)
Payables (money you owe people)	_____
Bank Loans (money you owe a bank)	_____
Car Loan	_____
Mortgages (home loan to bank)	_____
Credit card debt	_____
Total Liabilities	$_____

Total Assets $_____
minus Total Liabilities $_____
= Your Net Worth $_____

Net worth is what you OWN minus what you OWE!

THE POWER OF PHILANTHROPY

Principle/ Lesson:	Helping others is helping ourselves. Donating to help others is easy when you have an abundance mind-set.
What:	Philanthropy is the act of giving to others. When you give of yourself, whether with your time, energy, or dollars, it is returned to you in many forms at some other time. It's important not to give to get back though! You give and help because it feels good and makes the world a better place for everyone.
Why:	Teaching children to donate their money and time is a way to continue promoting the idea that we all live together on Earth and can help each other in infinite ways. Believe it or not, people who have an abundant mind-set (believe there always enough of everything to go around), generally always have enough. Our financial beliefs come into play here because we tend to donate more money to help others when we have a solid belief that we always have plenty. When your child chooses to donate money (from their allowance or business or a financial gift from a family member), to buy food and clothing for others or volunteer to help in a hospital or animal shelter, they are learning how good it feels to help others and be of service.
How:	Ask your child to explain the definition of the words 'donation' and 'philanthropy' and then explore the next two questions of the activity.
Comments/ Extra activities:	Tell your child about your experience in terms of giving to others: • How it made you feel, • What it did for the other person(s) or organization, • How you chose who to help or what to contribute to.
Vocabulary:	Philanthropy, abundance, mind-set, well-being, charity, charitable, donations, charities, non-profit organizations.

THE POWER OF PHILANTHROPY

The definition of **PHILANTHROPY** is:

"The desire to improve the well-being of humankind,

as by charitable help or donations."

What do you think this means:

_____

_____

Why do you think philanthropy is important for both you and others?

_____

_____

_____

_____

List several charities or non-profit organizations or causes you'd like to help...

_____

_____

_____

_____

FOOD BANK

JOB AND INCOME IDEAS

Principle/ Lesson:	Earning money creates an income; Making money creates a life. Opportunity is EVERYwhere.
What:	Profitable ideas come usually have one thing in common... ...they solve some kind of problem.
Why:	Brainstorming ideas (also called story boarding) is a great way to come up with creative money making ideas. You can do this with friends, family members, school mates.
How:	This is a great activity to do with a group of kids or the whole family. Suggest that they look around and notice areas of life where people have problems. See if they can spot business opportunities where they might be helpful to others or create products that serve a need that many people seem to have. Tell the story of the 16-year-old Nintendo expert: A teenager became really good at playing a video game and decided to write a pamphlet about how to beat the game with the idea that other people may want to know how to win the game also. He sold the pamphlet on the internet for $8.00 each. Over one year, he sold 100,000 copies, making $800,000.
Comments/ Extra activities:	Talk to your child about the types of things that you did as a child to earn money. Look on the internet for job ideas for kids. If you have entrepreneurs in the family or good friends who have had profitable ideas and acted on them, ask if they'll let your child spend some time chatting with them about what they did, how they did it, why they did it, etc.
Vocabulary:	Brain storming, jobs, income.

Brainstorm ideas for jobs or other ways to make earn and make money during the summer and school year!

_____

_____

_____

_____

_____

_____

_____

What do you need to do to make this happen?

_____

_____

_____

_____

_____

FINANCIAL GOALS AND FUN GOALS

Principle/ Lesson:	Most people don't get what they want because they don't know what they want. What you focus on expands. If you don't know where you're going, any road will take you there.
What:	Financial goals are just like any other goal...you need to know exactly what you want to create before you can set out to create it. There's a fun saying, Goals are simply dreams with a deadline! While not all goals are met on time (many aren't), at least having a projection or idea of when you'd like to accomplish a goal by really helps in the process. The other thing is to know is that not all people are 'goal-oriented'. Many, especially girls, are 'process-oriented.' This means they are more concerned and excited by the PROCESS of doing something than actually accomplishing something. It's good to know what kind of person you are early in life so you don't beat yourself up if you're not a goal person.
Why:	Setting goals is one of the main ways people accomplish things in life. Whether it's a college degree, a certain type of career, a lifestyle, setting up a grand purpose in life, goals are an integral part of the process. And goals change over the course of a lifetime. Getting children to learn and begin the habit of setting small, short-term goals (and dreaming, which they do naturally) is a great first step in helping them be successful in life.
How:	Ask your child what type of life he would like and how much money he would need to create for himself to live that type of life. Then ask him to think about a time line (by when) for accomplishing this. Help him walk through ways to accomplish this goal and lend ongoing support. Do the same thing with fun goals.
Comments/ Extra activities:	If he doesn't meet this goal (and any other goals), assure him that it's OK not to meet goals and that people modify goals all the time. It's just a guide from which to work. Share some goals you've set and accomplished and set, but didn't accomplish so he doesn't feel bad if he doesn't accomplish something by a certain time. Talk about the 'process' of reaching the goal as being more important than actually reaching the goal. If you lose sight of the road along the way, you've lost sight of life.
Vocabulary:	Financial goals, life-style, fun goals.

FINANCIAL GOALS AND FUN GOALS

Since we learned how important it is to set goals, set some for yourself:

What kind of life-style would you like to live when you're older (keeping in mind this changes often)? _____

_____

_____

How much money do you think it might take to life like this? _____

_____

By when would you like to accomplish this goal?_____

What are some of the things you need to do to meet this goal?

_____

_____

_____

And just for fun, list some other things you want to do?

_____

_____

_____

_____

Get a Goal Journal...keep adding to this list for the rest of your life. You are never too old to want to do things and create things!

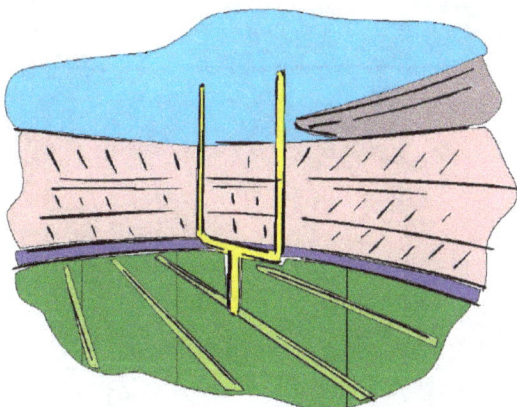

FINANCIAL FREEDOM IS YOUR CHOICE	
Principle/ Lesson:	Financial freedom is your choice. You are the CEO of your own life. Financial freedom is your choice. Most people don't get what they want because they don't know what they want.
What:	Financial freedom is a choice BUT you have to know two things: 1) that it IS a choice and 2) that you have to choose it. There are plenty of options you can choose and how you end up financially is an important choice most people never take the time to make, usually because no one ever teaches them it's an option.
Why:	Most people are never taught, and therefore never learn, that financial freedom is something they can, and must, choose for themselves. Too many human beings grow up thinking that they are at the affect of life when nothing could be further than the truth. Our thoughts, beliefs, choices...they all affect where our life takes us. If we knew this when we were young, most of us would have spent more time thinking and designing the exact lives we wanted to live.
How:	This is just a simple illustrated review page. On the left are expensive choices that make reaching financial freedom more challenging and don't necessarily bring joy, passion, or fulfillment. On the right are the three pillars of wealth...real estate, stock market and business ...which produce cash flow that leads to being financially free. Have your child fill in the blank (choice).
Comments/ Extra activities:	Talk to your child about whether or not you made the choice to be financially free and how making the choice, or not, affected your financial decisions along the way.
Vocabulary:	Financial freedom, mailbox income, choice.

FINANCIAL FREEDOM:

Is My _____!

Expensive Cars with big car payments and insurance costs.

Piddlyjunk that decreases in value when you buy it!

Huge Homes with large monthly payments

Real Estate

Stock Market

Business

Mailbox Income

FINANCIAL FREEDOM CONTRACT	
Principle/ Lesson:	I choose to be financially free. You are the CEO of your own life.
What:	Financial freedom is a choice and the responsibility for making it happen belongs with each individual once they make that choice.
Why:	Succeeding at anything is virtually impossible unless you set it as a goal first and choose it.
How:	Have your child read the page and if they choose to be financially free, have him or her (or them) sign and date it. You could tear out and frame this page and put it on the child's wall as well as a reminder to think about this every day.
Comments/ Extra activities:	Have a conversation about what he/she can do now to start learning more about money, saving money, etc.
Vocabulary:	Do-it-yourself project, financial freedom.

"If I'd known life was a do-it-yourself project I'd have started a long time ago!"

I Choose to be Financially Free!

_____   _____
Your Signature   Date

401(K) – Retirement plan offered by a for-profit company that allows its employees to set aside money tax deferred for retirement purposes. Some companies will match employees' contributions.

Abundance - The concept or belief that there is enough to go around, enough for everyone.

Appreciation – Increase in value of an asset.

Assets – A valuable item that is owned.

Asset Allocation – How an investor divides money in different asset classes such as stocks, bonds, cash, and real estate.

Amortization – The repayment of a loan in regular amounts over time.

ATM cards (Automated Teller Machine) - A plastic card issued by a bank or other financial institution to a person who has an account at that bank. It enables the account holder to deposit and withdraw money from their account at an ATM machine.

Balance - The amount of money your bank statement says you have in your account at the end of each month. Doesn't mean that's what's in your account right now though!

Bank Statement - A form you get from the bank each month that shows you how much money you have in your account as of the date on the statement, how much you put into your account that month, how much you took out of your account that month (withdrawals, checks, ATM, debit card purchases) and any fees you paid.

Balance sheet – Lists the value of assets, liabilities, and net worth of a person or company.

Bear market – A prolonged period in which stock prices fall accompanied by widespread pessimism.

Board of Directors – Individuals elected by a corporation's shareholders to oversee the management of the corporation.

Bond – Investment involving lending money to governments (city or national) or corporations. It has a face value (the amount it is worth when it matures), a fixed interest rate, and a fixed maturity date (when the bond holder receives the face value of the bond).

Borrowing - When someone gives you something to use that you must give back.

Budget – A forecast of your income and expenses expected for some time in the future. This is also known as your SSP or Savings and Spending Plan.

Bull market – A prolonged period in which stock prices rise faster than the historical average.

Capital – Wealth in the form of cash or goods used to generate income. Also, the net worth of a company (assets minus liabilities) is also called capital.

Cash flow – A measure of a company's financial health. It equals cash taken in less cash paid out over a given period of time. It is also called net worth.

CEO – Stands for chief executive officer – usually the president of a company.

CFO – Stands for chief financial officer – the executive responsible for the financial planning and record keeping for a company.

Certificate of Deposit (CD) – A low risk, low return investment offered by banks or savings and loans. It is also called a "time deposit" because the investor has agreed to keep the money in the account for a specified period of time – 3 months to six years. There is a monetary penalty for taking the money out before its maturity.

Charge Card - A type of credit card that requires you to pay your monthly balance in full at the end of each month. Charge cards generally have yearly fees and often don't have a hard credit limit. Instead, they estimate what they think their customers can afford to repay each month. American Express is one of the only companies that offers charge cards.

Check - A form of payment for a purchase that tells the person or business you wrote the check to that you have the money in your account so when they deposit your check into their account, the bank will transfer that amount of money into their account to complete the purchase.

Collateral – Property (land, house, stocks and bonds, car, jewelry, art, etc.) of value used to secure or guarantee a loan. If the loan is not paid, the lender can take the property (collateral) as payment instead.

Collectibles – Items such as baseball cards, antiques, or coins that have value due to their rarity or desirability.

Commission – A fee charged by a broker or agent for his/her services in helping with a transaction such as buying stock or real estate.

Compound Interest – Interest paid on the original deposit plus accumulated interest of prior periods, i.e., when your interest earns interest.

Corporation – A form of business organization that is granted a charter by a state giving it legal rights as an entity separate from its owners. It is characterized by the limited liability of its owners and the issuance of shares of stock.

Credit – A person's ability to borrow money.

Credit cards – Cards used to borrow money or buy goods and services, with the promise of paying later. Credit card purchases include interest if not paid by the due date each month.

Custodian – Agent, bank or trust company that holds and safeguards an individual's assets for them.

Debit cards - Similar to a check, a debit card is a promise that the recipient will be paid out of your bank account immediately, electronically. As it is taken directly from funds in your bank account, no debt is incurred.

Debt – An IOU or an obligation to pay. Bonds are debt instruments.

Default – Failure to pay back money on a timely basis that you borrowed from another.

Delayed Gratification - The ability to put off making a purchase until one saves up for it.

Depreciation – Decrease in value of an asset.

Demand - When the public wants a product or service. Works hand in hand with "supply."

Discount broker – One who charges lower commission rates than a full service broker but provides fewer services such as research and advice.

Dividend - A piece of the profits that some companies decide to pass on to their stockholders.

Diversification – Investing in a wide variety of investments to reduce your overall risk since some investments may perform better than others at any given time.

Dollar cost averaging – Investing the same amount of money on a regular schedule regardless of the price. For example, buying $25.00 worth of McDonald's stock every month. Stock prices may move up or down, but when you spread your purchase out like this, you get more shares when the price is down. Thus you buy most of your shares at a price lower than the average price.

Down payment – The part of the purchase price for a house/car or other large purchase that the buyer pays in cash, up front before he obtains a mortgage or loan on the remaining balance. Normally the larger the down payment (greater than 20%), the better interest rates you can get on a mortgage.

DRIP – (dividend reinvestment plan) - Automatically buys more shares of stock with profits without paying brokerage commissions.

Earned income – Income from paid employment, such as wages, salaries, tips, commissions, and bonuses as opposed to income from an investment that is unearned.

Earnings – The amount that is left of a corporations sales (revenue) after they have paid all of their expenses.

Earnings per share (EPS) – The total earnings of a company divided by their number of shares outstanding. EPS can be determined for any previous year (called trailing EPS), the current year (called current EPS), or for the future (called forward EPS). The last two would be estimates.

Expenses - Things that cost you money, i.e., in a business, expenses would include office rent, paper supplies, advertising, etc. At home, expenses would include rent or your house payment, food, insurance, gas, etc. Business expenses are often tax deductible.

FDIC – (Federal Deposit Insurance Corporation) - An agency of the U.S. government, established in 1933, that insures deposits up to $100,000 if the bank defaults (goes out of business).

Financial Freedom or Independence – When your monthly income exceeds the monthly expenses of your chosen lifestyle. Not being dependent on anyone else for your financial expenses: housing, transportation, food, etc.

Financial planner – An investment professional trained to help you plan and reach your long-term financial goals through investments, tax planning, asset allocation, retirement planning, and estate planning.

Financial statement – A written report that quantitatively describes your financial health at any given point in time. This includes what you own (assets) minus what you owe (liabilities) (a balance sheet), and your income and expense (an income statement). You must prepare a financial statement when you wish to qualify for a loan.

Gross Pay - The total amount of your paycheck before taxes and other deductions are taken out.

Index Fund – A type of mutual fund that attempts to mimic the performance of a particular index (such as the S & P 500) by buying similar amounts of similar stocks as that index consists of.

Inflation – The technical term for a rise in prices. Inflation usually occurs when there is too much money in circulation and not enough goods and services. Due to this excess demand, prices rise.

Insurance – A promise of compensation for specific potential future unexpected loss or injury in exchange for a periodic payment (e.g., health insurance, car insurance, home owner insurance, life insurance).

Interest – 1) A fee charged by a lender for the use of borrowed money, or 2) The return on an investment.

Interest-compound – Interest paid on the original deposit plus accumulated interest of prior periods, i.e., when your interest makes interest.

Interest-simple – Interest on the original deposit only.

Investing - When you put your money to work for you (see investment).

Investment – The outlay of money to purchase assets such as stocks, bonds, real estate or a business with the objective of making a profit when sold or receiving an income from dividends, interest, or rent while it is owned.

Investor - One who makes a business of investing in stocks, real estate, business, etc.

IPO – Initial Public Offering – the first time a company's stock is sold to the public.

IRA – (Individual Retirement Account) A retirement account that allows you to invest a set amount of money each year (used to be $2000, is now $3000 federal) where it will earn interest and/or dividends on a tax-deferred basis. You may begin withdrawing the money when you are 59½ years old. Withdrawing before that time incurs a 10% penalty.

IRS - (Internal Revenue Service.) The agency that is responsible for collecting our federal income taxes.

Leverage – The degree to which an investor or business is using borrowed money to operate. If a person or company is highly leveraged they run the risk of not being able to make payments on their debt. Using other people's time, energy and money to make you money.

Liability/liabilities – What you owe; a financial obligation or debt.

Loan – Money or property given to a borrower wit the agreement that the borrower will return the property or repay the money, usually with interest, at a specified time.

Maturity date – Date a loan must be paid back.

Millionaire - A person whose net worth (their assets minus their liabilities or what they own minus what they owe) is at least one million dollars.

Money market fund – Type of mutual fund that buys short-term, low risk securities. The main goal is the preservation of the principal. It usually offers a higher rate of interest than bank checking or savings accounts and the money is very accessible. Most of these accounts are not FDIC insured.

Mutual fund – A fund operated by an investment company that collects money from shareholders and invests it in a group of assets as determined by that funds objective. Fidelity is an investment company and Magellan is a mutual fund with a "large growth" objective.

NAIC – (National Association of Investors Corporation) A non-profit organization designed to help investors create or join investment clubs. This organization offers a variety of investment-related publications, online newsletters, software and videos that provide information on the investing process.

NASDAQ – (National Association of Security Dealers Automated Quotation System) A computerized system that facilitates the trading of stocks. Unlike the NYSE, the NASDAQ does not have a physical trading place that brings actual buyers and sellers together.

Needs - Things in life you have to have to life, i.e., food, water, air, transportation, housing.

Net asset value – The current market value of a single mutual fund share, calculated daily.

Net Pay - The amount of your paycheck after taxes and other deductions have been taken out.

Net worth – Total assets minus total liabilities.

No load – Mutual fund that does not charge a sales fee (load).

NSF - Stands for insufficient funds, i.e., if you write a check and don't have enough money in your account to cover it you will get a NSF notice and be charged NSF fees.

NYSE (New York Stock Exchange) – The oldest and largest stock exchange in the United States, it still uses a large trading floor (located on Wall Street in New York City) where representatives (called brokers) of buyers and sellers conduct transactions.

Passive income – Income received from business investments or real estate in which an individual is not actively involved, such as rent from an apartment building.

PE Ratio – Price per Earnings ratio – A common measure of how much investors are paying for the earnings of a company. A PE of 25 means investors are paying $25.00 for every dollar of earnings.

Pension – A benefit (money or compensation) offered by some employers and received after a person retires. These plans generally pay you a monthly income based upon your years of service with the employer.

Philanthropy – Increasing the well being of humankind by charitable aid or donations.

Points – A finance charge paid by the borrower at the beginning of a loan. One point is the same as one percent of the loan amount.

Portfolio – A collection of one's investments (stocks, bonds, mutual funds, real estate).

Portfolio income – The income received from the investments in a portfolio.

Principal - The amount of money borrowed or the part of the amount borrowed that is still owed. In investing, the principal is the amount of the original investment.

Profit - The money a business makes after it pays all its expenses.

Prospectus – A disclosure document telling the details of the mutual fund shares or stock of the company that issues it. The purpose of the prospectus information is to help an individual decide if the investment is right for him/her.

Reconcile – (same as balance) – To make sure your banking records (normally for a checking account) match your monthly bank statement.

Register - What you keep track of your spending in, e.g., checks you write, debit card purchases, deposits, withdrawals, etc.

Retirement – The point at which a person chooses to stop working full time for money. Legal age to receive federal social security payments is 62 and the amount you get increases if you retire at a later age. There are many younger people who have created financial freedom for themselves and say they are retired so retirement doesn't have an age attached to it anymore.

Rich - A word some people use to describe someone that has a lot of value, i.e., a millionaire might be considered rich; a piece of chocolate cake might be considered rich!

R.O.I. (Return on Investment) - The profit that you make on an investment, expressed as a percentage. If you put $1000 into an investment and one year later it's worth $1,100 you have made a profit of $100. Your ROI is your profit ($100) divided by the initial investment ($1000) or 10%.

Rule of 72 – The method used to determine how fast your money will double at a given interest rate. Money earning 6% will double in 12 years. 72 divided by the interest rate equals the number of years it will take for you to double your money.

Salary - A set amount of money you are paid each month for your job.

Saving - The act of accumulating something.

Savings account – An account in which the money earns interest but cannot be withdrawn by check writing.

Scarcity – An insufficient supply of something; the philosophy that there isn't enough to go around.

Security – Tradable document, such as stocks or bonds, which shows evidence of debt or ownership, such as a share of a business.

Share (same as a stock certificate) – A certificate representing one unit of ownership in a corporation, mutual fund, or limited partnership.

Social security – A government program that provides workers and their dependents with retirement income or disability income. The social security tax on wages is used to pay for this program.

Supply and demand – The concept that the price of an item is determined by the point at which the quantity available (supply) equals the quantity demanded. The price of an item will usually rise if there is more demand for the item than there is quantity available (Tickle-Me-Elmo a few years ago). Prices will usually fall if there is more of an item available than there is demand for it (department store sales).

Stock – An instrument that shows ownership in a corporation and represents a claim on a percentage of the corporation's assets and liabilities. The percentage is determined by the number of shares owned in relation to how many share exist.

Stock certificate - A document that represents ownership in a corporation.

Tax – An amount of money levied by a government on a product or a person's income. There are various kinds of taxes such as income tax, sales tax, gasoline tax, and property tax. Taxation funds government services such as road improvement, public educations, and street cleaning.

Tax deferred – Earnings from an investment normally that do not get taxed until the year in which you use the money (see IRA).

Tax exempt (same as tax free) – Earnings from an investment that never get taxed. Some cities issue bonds that earn interest tax-free.

Tithing – Giving a percentage of one's income as a donation, usually on a regular basis, to a worthy cause, such as a church, a mission, or Green Peace. Also known as donating or giving or philanthropy.

Total return – The amount received from an investment, including dividends, interest, and the appreciation or depreciation in the price, over a given period of time.

Treasury bills – (T-bills) – United States government debt obligations that mature in one year or less and are exempt from state and local taxes. They are low risk since they are backed by the government. Bills and bonds are one way in which the government raises money for its projects.

Treasury bonds – A coupon-bearing long-term debt instrument issued by the US government ranging from 10-30 years maturity issued in minimum denominations of $1000. Interest is paid by redeeming a coupon every six months.

Value - When someone feels like something is worth something. Something 'has value' or is 'valuable'.

Values - Usually refers to a person's morals or ethics or beliefs.

Volatility – A measure of the price movement of a security or the stock market in general. If prices move up and down quickly over short periods of time, the stock has high volatility. If the price rarely changes, it has low volatility.

Void - When you write a check and mess it up and need to destroy it you write VOID in the checkbook register or sometimes write VOID on the check itself.

Wall Street – A common name for the financial district in New York City and the street where the New York and American Stock Exchanges are located.

Wants - The stuff in life we don't necessarily need but have a desire for, i.e., a new bike or car, going on vacation, new clothes, a new stereo.

Withholding tax – Amount of an employee's income that is an employer sends directly to the federal and state governments as partial payment of an individual's tax liability for the year.

Yield – The annual rate of return on an investment expressed as a percentage, similar to ROI.

THANK YOU SO MUCH INVESTING YOUR HARD EARNED TIME, ENERGY AND MONEY IN YOUR CHILD'S FINANCIAL FUTURE! MAY THE REWARDS BE EXPERIENCED BY ALL.

FOR MORE AMAZING FINANCIAL EDUCATION RESOURCES

VISIT...

WWW.CAMPMILLIONAIRE.COM
WWW.WINTHEMONEYGAME.COM
WWW.FINANCIALEDUCATIONSTORE.COM
WWW.MONEYBOOKFORKIDS.COM
WWW.FINANCIALCOLORINGBOOKS.COM

CALL...

805-637-7888

EMAIL...

ELISABETH DONATI@GMAIL.COM

* 9 7 8 0 9 7 7 4 6 1 8 6 8 *